FINANCIAL INSTITUTIONS AND SERVICES

THE U.S. CREDIT REPORTING SYSTEM

ELEMENTS, INFRASTRUCTURE, AND KEY PROCESSES

FINANCIAL INSTITUTIONS AND SERVICES

Additional books in this series can be found on Nova's website under the Series tab.

Additional E-books in this series can be found on Nova's website under the E-book tab.

FINANCIAL INSTITUTIONS AND SERVICES

THE U.S. CREDIT REPORTING SYSTEM

ELEMENTS, INFRASTRUCTURE, AND KEY PROCESSES

KENDRICK A. MINOR
EDITOR

nova publishers
New York

Library of Congress Cataloging-in-Publication Data

ISBN: 978-1-62618-308-7

Published by Nova Science Publishers, Inc. † New York

CONTENTS

PREFACE

This book describes the credit reporting infrastructure at the three largest nationwide consumer reporting agencies (NCRAs), Equifax Information Services LLC, TransUnion LLC, and Experian Information Solutions Inc., with a special focus on the infrastructure and processes currently used by the NCRAs to collect, compile, and report information about consumers in the form of credit reports. Credit reports play an increasingly important role in the lives of American consumers. Most decisions to grant credit, including mortgage loans, auto loans, credit cards, and private student loans, include information contained in credit reports as part of the lending decision. These reports are also used in other spheres of decision making, including eligibility for rental housing, setting premiums for auto and homeowners insurance in some states, or determining whether to hire an applicant for a job. As the range and frequency of decisions that rely on credit reports have increased, so has the importance of assuring the accuracy of these reports.

Chapter 1 – This paper describes the credit reporting infrastructure at the three largest nationwide consumer reporting agencies (NCRAs) – Equifax Information Services LLC (Equifax), TransUnion LLC (TransUnion), and Experian Information Solutions Inc. (Experian) – with a special focus on the infrastructure and processes currently used by the NCRAs to collect, compile, and report information about consumers in the form of credit reports.

Credit reports play an increasingly important role in the lives of American consumers. Most decisions to grant credit – including mortgage loans, auto loans, credit cards, and private student loans – include information contained in credit reports as part of the lending decision. These reports are also used in other spheres of decision-making, including eligibility for rental housing, setting premiums for auto and homeowners insurance in some states, or determining whether to hire an applicant for a job.

As the range and frequency of decisions that rely on credit reports have increased, so has the importance of assuring the accuracy of these reports. These three NCRAs occupy the hub of what can best be described as a national credit reporting system. They, the entities who report information about borrowers to them (furnishers), providers of public records information, and consumers all play roles which affect the accuracy of the information reported in consumer credit reports.

In its supervision of large banks, the Consumer Financial Protection Bureau (CFPB) has already begun examining the processes institutions use to assure accuracy when furnishing information to the NCRAs and when responding to consumer disputes about information contained in their credit reports. On July 20, 2012 the CFPB published its larger participant rule permitting it to supervise companies with annual receipts from "consumer reporting," as defined in the rule, of over $7 million. Prior to the rule's effective date, the CFPB's Office of Deposits, Cash, Collections and Reporting Markets (DCCR) consulted existing reports, industry, and public sources in order to be able to depict key dimensions of, and processes in, the reporting and disputing of information in the U.S. credit reporting system.

This paper summarizes learnings from DCCR's research and analysis. It is intended as a public service to provide basic descriptions of, and statistics regarding, the underlying processes by which consumer data is reported, matched to consumer files, and reviewed when consumers dispute its accuracy. The CFPB has not sought to verify information contained in this paper through its supervisory authorities. Nor does the paper represent any learnings or conclusions about whether any specific market participants are in compliance with particular statutes or policies pertaining to consumer reporting.

This paper depicts the types of information movements and processes that are most essential to the compiling of credit reports and to the management of credit report accuracy. The Fair Credit Reporting Act (FCRA) and its implementing regulations impose legal duties both on NCRAs and on data furnishers relating to the accuracy of credit report information.[1] All parties to the credit reporting system have a vital interest in achieving accuracy in credit reports. Those who use these reports to make decisions rely upon the accuracy of the information they receive. To the extent the information is inaccurate, that can lead to incorrect decisions to the detriment of decision makers and consumers alike.

Chapter 2 – Prepared Remarks on Credit Reporting by Richard Cordray, Director of the Consumer Financial Protection Bureau. Presented at the Credit Reporting Field Hearing in Detroit, Michigan on July 16, 2012.

Chapter 3 – The purpose of the Fair Credit Reporting Act (FCRA) is "to require that consumer reporting agencies adopt reasonable procedures for meeting the needs of commerce for consumer credit, personnel, insurance, and other information in a manner which is fair and equitable to the consumer, with regard to the confidentiality, accuracy, relevancy, and proper utilization of such information." The FCRA establishes consumers' rights in relation to their credit reports, as well as permissible uses of credit reports. It also imposes certain responsibilities on those who collect, furnish, and use the information contained in consumers' credit reports.

The FCRA has been amended several times over the last decade. The Fair and Accurate Credit Transactions Act of 2003 (FACT Act, P.L. 108-159) amended the FCRA to include a number of provisions aimed at preventing identity theft and assisting victims. The Credit Card Accountability Responsibility and Disclosure Act of 2009 (Credit CARD Act, P.L. 111-24) strengthened protections for young consumers and advertising disclosures regarding free credit reports from consumer reporting agencies. More recently, the Consumer Financial Protection Act of 2010, part of the Dodd-Frank Wall Street Reform and Consumer Protection Act (P.L. 111-203), established the Consumer Financial Protection Bureau and transferred administrative functions, including most rulemaking and reporting, as well as certain enforcement functions, from other federal agencies, such as the Federal Trade Commission and the Federal Reserve Board, to the Bureau.

This report discusses consumers' rights under the FCRA, as well as the type of information included in credit reports, permissible uses of credit reports, disclosure requirements, and requirements for users of consumer credit reports and furnishers of information. It also addresses FCRA provisions aimed at preventing identity theft and assisting victims of identity theft.

Chapter 4 – The Federal Trade Commission ("FTC") and the Board of Governors of the Federal Reserve System ("Board") submit this report pursuant to section 313(b) of the Fair and Accurate Credit Transactions Act of 2003 ("the FACT Act"). The report discusses the steps that consumer reporting agencies ("CRAs") and furnishers of information to CRAs ("furnishers") take after receiving a consumer dispute about the accuracy or completeness of information in the consumer's file. The report first provides background information and describes the Fair Credit Reporting Act's ("FCRA's") dispute provisions. The core portion of the report, titled "The

Dispute Process," addresses (1) how the consumer submits a dispute to the CRA, (2) how the CRA forwards the dispute to the furnisher, (3) how the furnisher investigates the dispute and replies to the CRA, and (4) how the CRA reviews the furnisher's response and conveys the results of the reinvestigation to the consumer. The report also discusses the dispute process when consumers submit disputes directly to furnishers. The Board issued a request for public comment, and the report summarizes commenters' overall views on the dispute process.

The report finds that, although the materials that the FTC and the Board reviewed indicated that most disputes seem to be processed within the statutory time frame, there is disagreement as to the adequacy of the CRAs' and furnishers' investigations.

The FACT Act imposes a number of new requirements to enhance the consumer dispute process. These provisions are still being implemented. As a result, this report is based solely on compliance with the pre-FACT Act FCRA dispute process and recommends no additional administrative or legislative action at this time. The FTC and the Board believe that the FACT Act requirements should be given time to take effect before legislators and regulators consider making additional changes to the dispute process. The FTC and the Board will continue to monitor the performance of the dispute process, explore possible enhancements, and make recommendations for action, if appropriate.

In: The U.S. Credit Reporting System
Editor: Kendrick A. Minor

ISBN: 978-1-62618-308-7

Chapter 1

Key Dimensions and Processes in the U.S. Credit Reporting System: A Review of How the Nation's Largest Credit Bureaus Manage Consumer Data*

Consumer Financial Protection Bureau

Purpose and Executive Summary

This paper describes the credit reporting infrastructure at the three largest nationwide consumer reporting agencies (NCRAs) – Equifax Information Services LLC (Equifax), TransUnion LLC (TransUnion), and Experian Information Solutions Inc. (Experian) – with a special focus on the infrastructure and processes currently used by the NCRAs to collect, compile, and report information about consumers in the form of credit reports.

Credit reports play an increasingly important role in the lives of American consumers. Most decisions to grant credit – including mortgage loans, auto loans, credit cards, and private student loans – include information contained in credit reports as part of the lending decision. These reports are also used in other spheres of decision-making, including eligibility for rental housing,

* This is an edited, reformatted and augmented version of the Consumer Financial Protection Bureau, dated December 2012.

setting premiums for auto and homeowners insurance in some states, or determining whether to hire an applicant for a job.

As the range and frequency of decisions that rely on credit reports have increased, so has the importance of assuring the accuracy of these reports. These three NCRAs occupy the hub of what can best be described as a national credit reporting system. They, the entities who report information about borrowers to them (furnishers), providers of public records information, and consumers all play roles which affect the accuracy of the information reported in consumer credit reports.

In its supervision of large banks, the Consumer Financial Protection Bureau (CFPB) has already begun examining the processes institutions use to assure accuracy when furnishing information to the NCRAs and when responding to consumer disputes about information contained in their credit reports. On July 20, 2012 the CFPB published its larger participant rule permitting it to supervise companies with annual receipts from "consumer reporting," as defined in the rule, of over $7 million. Prior to the rule's effective date, the CFPB's Office of Deposits, Cash, Collections and Reporting Markets (DCCR) consulted existing reports, industry, and public sources in order to be able to depict key dimensions of, and processes in, the reporting and disputing of information in the U.S. credit reporting system.

This paper summarizes learnings from DCCR's research and analysis. It is intended as a public service to provide basic descriptions of, and statistics regarding, the underlying processes by which consumer data is reported, matched to consumer files, and reviewed when consumers dispute its accuracy. The CFPB has not sought to verify information contained in this paper through its supervisory authorities. Nor does the paper represent any learnings or conclusions about whether any specific market participants are in compliance with particular statutes or policies pertaining to consumer reporting.

This paper depicts the types of information movements and processes that are most essential to the compiling of credit reports and to the management of credit report accuracy. The Fair Credit Reporting Act (FCRA) and its implementing regulations impose legal duties both on NCRAs and on data furnishers relating to the accuracy of credit report information.[1] All parties to the credit reporting system have a vital interest in achieving accuracy in credit reports. Those who use these reports to make decisions rely upon the accuracy of the information they receive. To the extent the information is inaccurate, that can lead to incorrect decisions to the detriment of decision makers and consumers alike.

KEY LEARNINGS

- **The U.S. credit reporting system encompasses a vast flow and store of information.** The NCRAs each maintain credit files on over 200,000,000 adults and receive information from approximately 10,000 furnishers of data. On a monthly basis, these furnishers provide information on over 1.3 billion consumer credit accounts or other "trade lines."
- **Furnishing credit information to the NCRAs is a highly concentrated activity, both by institution and by product.** The 10 largest institutions furnishing credit information to each of the NCRAs account for more than half of all accounts reflected in consumers' credit files. Likewise, retail and network-branded revolving credit cards account for nearly 60% of all trade lines.
- **The NCRAs have designed a number of processes to standardize, automate, and perform quality controls on incoming data.** The NCRAs report that before accepting information from data furnishers, they perform certain background and quality control checks on would-be-furnishers. Most furnishers – and all new furnishers – provide consumer credit information electronically to one or more NCRAs using a standardized format called Metro 2 that the Consumer Data Industry Association (CDIA) developed and refined over time. When data files are received, the NCRAs also perform quality checks prior to adding the data to credit files.
- **The "matching" process by which the NCRAs assign incoming trade line data to consumer-specific credit files represents the central step in the organization of credit data to permit the creation of credit reports on individual consumers.** The NCRAs manage this process through unique data architectures each has developed and which vary from each other. The challenge of accurately matching trade line information to the correct consumer is made complex by the absence of any objective, third party source of information, by similarities in consumers' names and addresses (particularly among family members), and by limitations, colloquial variations, and inaccuracies in the personally identifying information provided by consumers and furnishers that occur when consumers first apply for credit products.
- **Inaccuracies can enter into credit reports in a number of ways.** Inaccuracies can occur if consumers provide inaccurate data when

applying for a loan or if the creditor who furnishes data to the credit bureau inputs consumer information to its systems inaccurately. Inaccuracies can occur when the bureaus match information about a consumer from a particular data furnisher to the wrong individual consumer's file. Inaccuracies can also come from errors or the lack of identifying information in government records. Inaccuracies can occur when consumers have become victims of identity fraud or identity theft.

- **The extent to which credit reports contain material inaccuracies is uncertain.** There have been conflicting reports on this issue. The Federal Trade Commission (FTC) is expected to release results from its decade-long study on credit report accuracy later this year.
- **Consumers' right to dispute information contained in their credit reports under the FCRA – and furnishers' and the NCRAs' obligation to respond – provide important checks on inaccurate credit reports.** Among other protections, consumers also have the right to obtain a copy of their credit file and to receive notice of adverse actions involving credit reports with a resultant right to a free disclosure. These disclosures are one way for consumers to dispute information in their file they believe is not accurate or complete. The CFPB estimates that at least 40,000,000 consumers obtain a copy of their credit file from one or more of the NCRAs annually.
- **The NCRAs received approximately 8 million contacts from consumers in 2011 to initiate disputes about the accuracy of one or more items on their credit files.** In total, these 8 million contacts resulted in 32 – 38 million disputed items on consumers' credit files. The rate at which the credit account information depicted in credit files is disputed varies widely based upon the type of data furnished.
- **Collections items are a major source of disputes.** Items reported by collection agencies reportedly have the highest dispute rates, averaging 1.1% of the trade lines they furnish in a given year. Almost 40% of disputes handled by the NCRAs on average can be linked to collections items.
- **The NCRAs have created an automated system for handling consumer disputes and forwarding them to data furnishers.** Through this automated system – called e- OSCAR – the NCRAs provide furnishers with one or two numeric codes indicating the nature of the consumer's dispute and in a minority of cases (26%), explanatory text. At present, the NCRAs generally do not forward

documentation that consumers submit with mailed disputes or provide a mechanism for consumers to forward supporting documents when filing disputes online or via phone. The NCRAs resolve an average of 15% of trade line disputes internally (without furnisher involvement) and refer the remaining 85% of the disputes they receive from consumers concerning trade lines to data furnishers through e-OSCAR. The furnisher of the disputed data is then required by the FCRA to investigate the dispute and report back to the NCRA.

- **The NCRAs' reliance on furnisher responses as the principal means of resolving disputes is a source of controversy.** The NCRAs report that in seeking to maximize accuracy and in resolving disputes, they rely on furnishers meeting their obligations under the FCRA to report information accurately and to respond to disputes appropriately. Consumer advocates have argued that the NCRAs have an obligation to monitor and manage furnisher practices as part of their broader obligation to achieve credit report accuracy.
- **While the measurement of credit report accuracy and the level and causes of inaccuracies present challenges, periodic measurement of credit report accuracy holds promise for establishing baseline accuracy levels and measuring improvements over time.**

1. INTRODUCTION

In most of the markets for consumer credit, including credit cards, auto loans, mortgages, and student loans, lenders use credit reports as part of their evaluation of a consumer's application for credit. Companies use credit reports and credit scores derived from the information in credit reporting files to assess a consumer's likelihood of repaying the loan. Credit reports and scores can be delivered in real time, permitting instant decisions at retailers, auto showrooms, or online. Lists of consumers derived from credit reports are used to make offers of credit. Underwriting processes stipulated by the FHA, VA, Fannie Mae, and Freddie Mac require mortgage lenders to obtain credit reports from a nationwide credit reporting agency (the NCRAs) before these federal agencies and government-sponsored enterprises will insure, guarantee, or purchase their loans. For each of these forms of credit and origination channels, credit reports are used by lenders to help set interest rates and other key credit terms, or determine whether the consumer is offered credit at all. Of

113 million credit card and retail card accounts, auto loans, personal loans, mortgages, and home equity loans originated in the United States in 2011, the vast majority of approval decisions used information furnished by credit reporting agencies.[2]

Credit reports also are used in spheres of decision-making beyond eligibility for credit. These include eligibility for rental housing,[3] setting premiums for auto and other property and casualty insurance where permitted by law,[4] and establishing (along with prior account history) eligibility for checking accounts.[5] When an individual applies for a job, a prospective employer may examine his or her credit report upon the individual's authorization.[6] A recent survey by the Society for Human Resource Management of its membership database found that almost 60% of its member employers used credit reports to screen applicants for at least some of their positions.[7]

Because of the widespread use of credit reports – often along with credit scores derived from them – in major personal financial decisions, the accuracy of reports has remained an ongoing policy concern. In a 2007 report on credit scores used in lending decisions, the Federal Reserve Board noted the importance of accurate credit reports: "for the full benefits of the credit-reporting system to be realized, credit records must be reasonable, complete, and accurate."[8] Credit scoring models depend on the credit information contained in consumers' credit files to be accurate to effectively predict a consumer's relative risk of delinquency. Inaccurate credit information may cause credit scoring models to understate or overstate a consumer's credit risk to lenders. Accurate credit information helps decision makers predict certain risks effectively, while inaccurate credit information in credit reports has the potential to compromise the effectiveness and consistency of decisions that rely on them, and the potential to cause material harm to affected consumers. Ultimately, consumer and business confidence in decisions based on credit reports and scores derived from them depends on confidence in the accuracy of the credit information they contain.[*]

When the FCRA passed in 1970, key provisions of the law focused on assuring the accuracy of credit reports. These key accuracy provisions of the

[*] The issues raised in this discussion of credit report accuracy also generally apply to consumer reports from consumer reporting agencies as defined under the FCRA. Besides the NCRAs, there are other consumer reporting agencies including the nationwide specialty consumer reporting agencies with rental information databases, check writing/bank databases, medical information databases, insurance claims databases, employment databases, and background screening databases. Each of these specialty databases has its own sources of consumer information. There are also consumer reporting agencies that are not nationwide.

FCRA remain as important today as when the law first passed. They address the quality of data in credit files by requiring credit reporting agencies to establish "reasonable procedures to assure maximum possible accuracy" of their credit reports.[9] The FCRA also includes a number of other provisions that relate to the information in consumer reports such as limits on the period of time during which certain pieces of adverse information can generally be included in a consumer report.[10]

Credit report accuracy relies on an ongoing ecosystem involving the interaction of NCRAs and other consumer reporting agencies, furnishers of information, public record repositories, users of credit reports, and consumers. An understanding of how this ecosystem operates – including the basic "plumbing" of data flows, the various participants involved, and the economic incentives each group of participants may bring to their respective roles – is foundational knowledge in considering technical and policy options for improving and assuring credit report accuracy.

This paper focuses on the databases of the three largest NCRAs – Equifax, TransUnion, and Experian. It seeks to depict technical processes involved in the collection, screening, and correction of credit information and their broad impact on the accuracy of information provided in credit reports from these NCRAs. It does not seek to characterize or quantify either the general *level* of accuracy of credit report information, or the harms that may result to consumers affected by credit report inaccuracies. Additionally, the paper does not attempt to weigh the costs and benefits that might be involved in improving the accuracy of credit reports beyond their current levels.

2. Credit Bureaus, Credit Files, Credit Reports, and Credit Scores

2.1. Credit Bureaus

The consumer reporting system enables creditors and other providers of consumer services to pool information about their respective customers and use that pooled information to inform their credit and other risk decisions about new applicants and existing customers.

Credit bureaus first emerged in the United States in the late 1800s to support merchant lenders who extended credit to local businesses and individuals.[11] At that time, the "credit bureau" consisted of a list of individuals who had not repaid their debts as agreed and were therefore deemed poor credit risks. Prior to the use of such lists, local merchants extended only very small amounts of credit, and these credit decisions depended largely on the merchant's direct personal knowledge of the individual borrower's personal character. The credit reporting industry grew steadily with growing interest on the part of both consumers and merchants in using credit in purchase transactions. In the 1920s and again in the 1950s, credit bureaus experienced particularly rapid growth with the introduction of retail installment credit and revolving credit accounts,[12] in the 1970s and 1980s with the growth of bank credit cards, and in the 1990s with the automation of mortgage underwriting. By the early 1970s, the industry comprised over 2,250 firms, most with local or regional coverage. As the 1970s progressed, the industry began to consolidate.[13] With the development of computer databases, nationwide credit card issuers, and automated underwriting, the threshold of technological investment required to distribute credit reports increased, as did the importance of offering nationwide coverage. Many of the local bureaus sold their records to the major national bureaus. Today, the consumer reporting landscape includes large national bureaus like the NCRAs; bureaus with credit information such as payday loans, utility and telephone accounts, and other credit relationships; a number of specialized consumer reporting agencies with medical information, employment history, residential history, check writing history, checking account history, insurance claims, and other non-credit relationships; as a well as a few hundred resellers of credit reports. By 2011, the NCRAs generated U.S. revenues of about $4 billion,[14] including revenues from several ancillary businesses such as the sale of lists and non-credit consumer information for marketing purposes, the sale of credit monitoring services directly to consumers or through resellers, and analytical services that provide credit scores and other modeling tools to creditors.

2.2. The Contents of Consumer Credit Files

For purposes of this paper, credit reports are a form of "consumer report" as defined by the FCRA. Consumer reports generally are communications by a consumer reporting agency "bearing on a consumer's credit worthiness, credit standing, credit capacity, character, general reputation, personal characteristics, or mode of living" used or expected to be used in determining a consumer's eligibility for credit or insurance, for employment purposes, or other permissible purposes listed in the statute.[15] As defined by the FCRA, the "file," when used in connection with information on any consumer, means "all of the information on that consumer recorded and retained by a consumer reporting agency regardless of how the information is stored."[16] This paper refers to "credit files" as the information about a consumer that is contained in the databases of the NCRAs.

2.2.1. File Components

Credit files have some or all of the following components.

1. ***Header/Identifying Information***: The header of a credit file contains the identifying information of the consumer with whom the credit file is associated including an individual's name (and any other names previously used), current and former addresses, Social Security number (SSN), date of birth, and phone numbers. Not all credit files contain all of these identifying elements.[17]
2. ***Trade lines***: Trade lines are the accounts in a consumer's name reported by creditors such as auto lenders, mortgage lenders, or credit card issuers. For each trade line, creditors that furnish information to consumer reporting agencies (referred to as "furnishers" under the FCRA) generally provide the type of credit (e.g., auto loan, mortgage, credit card), the credit limit or loan amount, account balance, the account payment history including the timeliness of payments, whether or not the account is delinquent or in collection, and the dates the account was opened and closed. If more than one consumer is listed as a borrower on a given credit account, the trade line information will appear in both consumers' credit files ordinarily with information as to the relationship of the consumer to the account, such as authorized user. Trade line information may contain indicators such as whether the account is individual or joint, the account is involved in a bankruptcy filing, the device for accessing the account (e.g., a credit card or PIN) was lost or stolen, and, if closed, the reason for closure (e.g., paid off, closed at the consumer's request). Credit files do not contain certain terms of the loans or credit lines such as interest rates, points, or fees and do not contain certain performance history such as purchases made using the account or payments made on the account. Additionally, credit reports do not contain information on a consumer's income or assets.
3. ***Public record information***: The NCRAs' files include public record data of a financial nature including consumer bankruptcies,

judgments, and state and federal tax liens. Records of arrests and convictions generally do not appear on a consumer's credit file, but other types of consumer reporting agencies, such as employment background screening agencies, include them. Other public records that do not appear in credit reports are marriage records, adoptions, and records of civil suits that have not resulted in judgments.[18]

4. ***Collections***: Third-party collection items, reported by debt buyers or collections agencies on behalf of a creditor, are considered a separate category on a credit report by at least some of the NCRAs.
5. ***Inquiries***: A consumer's credit file is required to list every entity that accessed the file in the last two years for employment-related uses and for at least the last year for credit uses and most non-employment uses (e.g., tenant screening, insurance, government licenses or benefits).[19] Some of the NCRAs go beyond legal requirements and list credit inquiries for two years.

   The NCRAs have two major classifications of inquiries: "soft" inquiries and "hard" inquiries. Hard inquiries are typically the product of consumer-initiated activities such as applications for credit cards, to rent an apartment, to open a deposit account, or for other services. In contrast, soft inquiries are generally user-initiated inquiries like prescreening.[*] Only hard inquiries will appear in credit reports obtained by creditors and other users.

A consumer's file also has information on whether the consumer has initiated a security freeze, fraud alert, active duty alert, or filed a consumer statement on his or her file.

2.3. Credit Reports

Credit reports are consumer reports provided by NCRAs or other CRAs to lenders and other users. Credit reports generally contain information in the consumer file that is reportable to the end user.

---

[*] The NCRAs treat other types of inquiries as soft inquiries based on business rules – certain insurance inquiries, utility, and government inquiries relating to licenses or government benefits may be categorized as soft, depending on the business rules for that entity. Employment inquiries are commonly placed in the soft inquiry section. Each listed inquiry will include the date and type of inquiry (e.g., by consumer, review of existing account, for pre-screening). Federal Trade Commission and the Federal Reserve Board, Report to Congress on the Fair Credit Reporting Act Dispute Process, at 4 (August 2006).

The FCRA limits with some exceptions how long a credit bureau can communicate certain adverse information in a credit report.[20] Many adverse items including records of late payments, delinquencies, or collection items typically stay on a credit report for up to seven years.[21] Likewise, civil suits and civil judgments typically stay on the report for no more than the longer of seven years or the governing statute of limitations, while paid tax liens typically cannot be reported more than seven years after the date of payment.[22] Credit reports generally cannot list bankruptcies for more than 10 years after the order for relief or date of adjudication, except that repayment plans are only reported for seven years.[23] There are also restrictions on communicating a medical service provider's name, address, and telephone number pertaining to medical debts in a credit report.[24]

Users vary in how they evaluate credit reporting information. For users who view reports for employment purposes, the NCRAs provide a modified credit report, which removes birth date and other information that is sensitive in the employment context and does not include credit scores. Financial services users rely on credit reports as well as proprietary or third-party algorithms – "scoring" models – to interpret the information in a credit report. These algorithms use variables or "attributes" derived from the credit report.

2.4. Credit Scoring

The NCRAs deliver credit reporting information to users in standardized electronic formats so that lenders' underwriting systems can use reports from more than one bureau interchangeably and so that analytical credit risk models used by the lenders can identify and retrieve relevant pieces of information. More often than not, a credit bureau will also deliver a credit score calculated from the information in a credit report along with variables derived from the credit report (often called attributes). [25] The lender will pay the bureau a fee for the credit report information and an additional amount for the score. The model used to generate the credit score is selected by the lender as the user.

Lenders use credit scoring systems to assess the relative risk of consumers going delinquent on a loan. For most credit scoring models in use today, the higher the numerical value of a credit score, the lower the credit risk of a consumer. Consumers with very high scores thus are likely to get more favorable interest rates and other more favorable loan terms. In contrast, consumers with lower numerical scores present higher risks of default and may only be able to get loans at higher interest rates or other less favorable terms, if lenders are willing to lend to them at all.

Large national lenders have widely used credit scoring since the 1970s to inform their loan underwriting.[26] The NCRAs did not start providing credit scores based on credit bureau data until the late 1980s. In the late 1980s, one bureau built a bankruptcy prediction model. Models supplied by Fair Isaac Corporation (FICO) for use with credit bureau data appeared in 1990 and 1991.

Today, scores using models supplied by FICO account for a substantial majority of third-party generic credit scores purchased with credit reports by financial institutions for loan origination decisions.[27] In 2006 the NCRAs formed a joint venture, VantageScore, which offers competing scoring solutions. Additionally, the NCRAs and other third-party development companies develop both generic and custom scoring models. Many lenders also develop and use proprietary scoring models derived from credit report information.

The most common credit scores rank the relative probability that a consumer will become 90 days delinquent on a new loan within two years. There are a wide variety of credit scores offered by the NCRAs that vary by score provider, by model, and by target industry.[28] FICO, alone, has 49 different scoring models.[29]

Regardless of the version, credit scoring models tend to share common "attributes" derived from credit reports, such as a consumer's bill paying history (e.g., on time, delinquent, in collections), the number and type of credit accounts a consumer has (e.g., bank cards, retail credit cards, installment loans), the amount of available credit that a consumer is using, how long a consumer has had a credit account, and recent credit activity, including inquiries.

Creditors use credit scores to enhance the efficiency and consistency of credit decisioning.[30] Credit scores may also reduce the possibility of subjective decision making by lenders based on impermissible factors under fair lending laws such as the Equal Credit Opportunity Act (ECOA), like marital status, age or national origin.

The Federal Reserve noted in its 2007 study on credit scoring, "By providing a low-cost, accurate, and standardized metric of credit risk for a pool of loans, credit scoring has broadened creditors' access to capital markets, reduced funding costs, and strengthened public and private scrutiny of lending activities."[31]

Some have argued that credit scores derived from credit reports have the potential to reinforce the effects of discrimination. They argue that where lending discrimination occurs, minority and other disadvantaged borrowers can wind up in credit products that make default more likely. As a result of higher default rates, their credit reports and scores depict them as bad credit risks, when in fact they would have performed better if they were in better, less expensive products.[32]

NCRAs can deliver credit reports and scores (using proprietary or third-party models) to those authorized to access a credit report instantly upon request.

This makes it possible for lenders to grant instant credit in venues where obtaining credit is often an important part of a consumer's purchase decision, such as at an auto dealer or a department store. Additionally, incorporating the use of credit scores as a factor in underwriting has enabled the government-sponsored entities, Fannie Mae and Freddie Mac, to introduce automated underwriting systems that allowed mortgage originators to streamline the mortgage underwriting process and provide rapid mortgage approvals.

Because credit scores are derived from the information in credit reports, inaccuracies in credit report information can affect consumers' credit scores. Some inaccuracies matter more than others.

An error in a consumer's address, the misspelling of a maiden name, or other errors in the consumer's identification information are generally unlikely to have an impact on a consumer's credit score or perceived credit worthiness by lenders.

However, a public record that inaccurately indicates a consumer is subject to a tax lien, or a trade line that incorrectly states a consumer had a severe delinquency, could cause a lender to deny credit to a consumer altogether, or to treat a consumer it would otherwise consider eligible for a loan at prime interest rates as only eligible for sub-prime rates, costing the consumer thousands of dollars in interest.

Below is a table showing how credit scores may be affected when specific adverse information appears in a credit report using different starting scores from VantageScore and FICO, two credit score providers. FICO scores generally have a range of 300 to 850, while Vantage scores range from 501 to 990.

It is worth noting that these score impacts are hypothetical, and that the impact of an adverse event in any individual's case varies by the unique characteristics of that consumer's credit history, including the number and timing of such events.

Other than credit scores, the NCRAs also provide lenders with analytical models using credit report data. These include models that predict the likelihood of accepting a credit offer, of future account utilization, of consumers leaving an existing account, or of collectability on an outstanding debt.

Financial Data	Score Impact Range			
	Consumer with 900 Vantage Score	**Consumer with 760 Vantage Score**	**Consumer with 780 FICO Score**	**Consumer with 680 FICO Score**
Bank card – 30 days delinquent	70-90 point drop	60-80 point drop	90-110 point drop	60-80 point drop
Mortgage charge-off or foreclosure	130-170 point drop	80-110 point drop	140-160 point drop	95-115 point drop
Filing bankruptcy	350+ point drop	200+ point drop	220-240 point drop	130-150 point drop

Sources: **VantageScore**: Sara Davies, Introduction to the VantageScore Model, Ways Consumer Credit Scores Are Impacted and Methods for Score Improvement, Presentation at the Symposium on Credit Scoring and Credit Reporting at Suffolk University Law School (June 6, 2012).

FICO: http://www.myfico.com/crediteducation/questions/Credit_Problem_ Compa rison. aspx.

Figure 1. Example Score Impacts.

3. Furnishers and Users

In addition to the NCRAs and other CRAs, the most important participants in the credit reporting system are *furnishers, users,* and *consumers*. All of these participants have defined roles with specific obligations under the FCRA.

Most furnishers of credit information to NCRAs are creditors who are also users of credit reports. Public records (e.g., judgments, bankruptcy filings, tax liens) are also important sources of information for NCRAs.

Figure 2 below is a simplified diagram of the information flows in the credit reporting system.

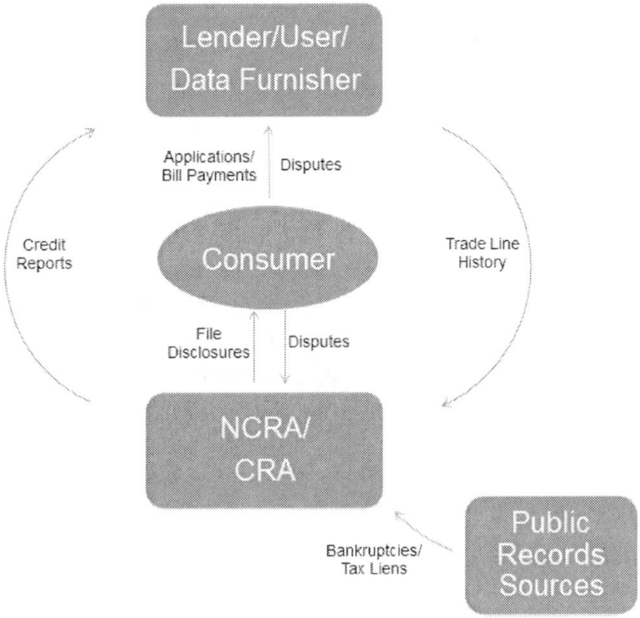

Source: CFPB 2012.

Figure 2. The Credit Reporting System.

3.1. Trade Line Furnishers

Each NCRA has a consumer database with over 1.3 billion active trade lines.[33] Financial institutions furnish the bulk of these trade lines. Approximately 40% of all trade lines of an NCRA's files are bank card trade lines. Of the remaining trade lines, 18% came from banks that issue retail cards, 13% are accounts in collection reported by collections agencies and debt buyers, 7% from the education industry,* 7% from sales finance providers (e.g., closed-end loans including auto loans), 7% from mortgage lenders or servicers, 4% from auto lenders, and 4% from other unspecified creditors.[34]

While the NCRAs receive trade lines from approximately 10,000 furnishers, a small number of very large institutions (typically with multiple lines of business) supply a majority of trade lines. For the NCRAs, the top 10

* Education furnishers are comprised of furnishers from business education schools, colleges, private educational lenders, technical education universities, vocational and trade schools, and government furnishers including the Department of Education and federal student loan servicers.

furnishers provide approximately 57% of the trade lines, the top 50 furnishers provide 72% of the trade lines, and the top 100 furnishers provide 76% of the trade lines in their databases.[35] The institutions' credit offerings can include bank credit cards, retailer credit cards, auto loans, student loans, and mortgages.[36] Other furnisher industries, such as collections agencies, tend to be more fragmented.[37]

Furnishers typically report trade line updates monthly in batch files transmitted electronically to one or more of the NCRAs. Most of the largest furnishers report all or nearly all of their trade lines to each of the largest NCRAs.[*] These updates generally include changes in balances owed, whether or not payments were received, changes in available credit lines (in the cases of revolving credit card accounts), and the status of the account (e.g., current, 30+ days late, 60+ days late). The NCRAs provide a standardized data format, called Metro 2, which most of their furnishers use to submit data.[†]

3.1.1. Furnisher Incentives and Disincentives

Reporting to credit bureaus and other consumer reporting agencies by creditors is voluntary and historically has been. Not all creditors report information about their borrowers. Some creditors report information about users of some of their credit products, but not others. For example, credit card issuers who issue revolving credit to consumers usually report trade line information monthly on consumer cards but are less likely to report on small business cards even when these are owed by, and underwritten based on, the personal credit history of the business owner.

Furnishers have multiple incentives to contribute data to the NCRAs. Individual contributors recognize that the cross-company, cross-industry visibility into credit risk offered by a credit bureau depends on widespread creditor participation. If a company elects not to contribute data, it runs the risk that its peers will not contribute data, thus reducing a common resource from which creditors benefit. As indicated above, most furnishers of trade line information to the NCRAs are also large users of credit reports.

A second reason creditors furnish information on their accounts is to maintain an incentive for their borrowers to make timely repayments.

[*] The NCRAs do have some variations in their source data. Some smaller banks and many debt collection agencies do not send information to all three of the largest NCRAs. See Federal Trade Commission and Federal Reserve Board, *Report to Congress on the Fair Credit Reporting Act Dispute Process*, at 5 (August 2006). .

[†] Innovis, a credit bureau, also is a participant in the Metro reporting system. It offers portfolio management solutions, fraud solutions, and authentication solutions, among other services.

Consumers are more likely to repay creditors if they are aware that a creditor may report late payments or delinquent accounts to the NCRAs, which could negatively affect their credit history and/or credit score. Consumers also get the benefit of having their timely payments reported, which will positively impact lenders' views of their credit worthiness.

There are also disincentives for creditors to report on their borrowers to the NCRAs.[38] For example, the names of individuals who borrow and make loan payments on time may be included in prescreened lists that NCRAs and other CRAs sell, providing these borrowers with account offers from competing lenders. Reporting to one or more of the NCRAs may require investment in specialized information systems. Further, data furnishers must follow FCRA requirements such as investigating disputes submitted directly[39] or indirectly through the NCRAs. Since furnishing data is voluntary, furnishers must consider whether the overall benefits of furnishing outweigh its costs.

3.1.2. Reporting Format

CDIA developed the Metro 2 guidelines in 1997, on behalf of the NCRAs and Innovis, as their standard for the electronic reporting of consumer trade line information. Metro 2 replaced the original Metro format developed in the late 1970s.[40] The format forms the basis by which furnishers provide updates on their borrowers' account status in bulk file submissions to one or more of the NCRAs, generally on a monthly basis. An obvious benefit of a shared data format is that all furnishers can report trade line information the same way. This simplifies the creation of standardized credit files by each of the NCRAs and simplifies the interpretation of credit information into risk-based credit scores.

Each Metro 2 electronic file submission has a furnisher header record, a series of base records on each borrower, supplementary records describing updates to the furnished trade lines, and a trailer record. A description of the various types of record segments and the information that Metro 2 allows furnishers to provide is offered below.

- **Metro 2 Header and Trailer Records**: Header and Trailer records form the bookends of a Metro 2 file submission. The header record is the first record provided in the Metro 2 file submission and is used to identify the furnisher and the activity period. It also contains the furnisher's unique identifier at the NCRA receiving the file, the activity date, name, address, and other contact information for the furnisher. Note that this type of header record should be distinguished from the header record on a consumer file maintained by an NCRA that has the consumer's personal identification information. The trailer record, meanwhile, is the last record in a furnisher's Metro 2 submission. It includes the sum totals of all the base and supplementary segments submitted.

- **Base Segment**: The Base segment is used to identify the primary borrower and to provide relevant account information for each trade line. Identification information for the borrower includes first, middle, last name, suffix, generation code, phone number, address, SSN, and date of birth. Account information includes account type (e.g., revolving, installment, mortgage), credit limit, highest credit or original loan amount, duration of credit extended, frequency with which payments are due, account status,* stage of delinquency, date of first delinquency, and date the account closed and conditions under which it was closed (e.g., closed by consumer, paid full amount due, closed by creditor and paid less than full amount). Additionally, the Base segment contains up to 24 months of the consumer's payment history on the account. Contrary to a frequent assumption, the Metro 2 format does not contain fields for interest rate information on particular loans or revolving accounts.
- **Supplementary Segments**: Depending on the furnisher and the type of trade line, the furnisher may have additional data segments to supplement the data in the base segment. These include:
  - **Associated Consumer Segment**: Contains information on consumers who are associated with a credit account besides the primary user, including name, SSN, date of birth, telephone number, and the relation of the consumer to the account. Associated consumers can include authorized users, guarantors, persons with joint contractual liability, or others.
  - **Original Creditor Name Segment**: Has the name of the original credit grantor, which is necessary to link a consumer debt to the original creditor even after it is outsourced to a third-party collection agency.

---

* Account status reflects the current or final disposition of the account. If the account is delinquent, Metro 2 allows furnishers to report the level of delinquency such as 30-59 days past due, 60-89 days past due, and up to 180 days or more past due. Where the account is closed, a furnisher can report whether the account closed with a zero balance, was a voluntary surrender, closure surrender, repossession, charge-off, or entered into foreclosure.

- **Segment for Accounts Sold to/Purchased from Another Company**: Used to report the name of the companies which respectively bought and sold a portfolio of consumer debt.
- **Mortgage Information**: Used to report any Fannie Mae or Freddie Mac loan number associated with a mortgage account.
- **Specialized Payment Information**: Has information on deferred payments or balloon payments, if applicable.
- **Account Number/Identification Number**: Used to report new identification or account numbers.
- **Employment Segment**: Contains employment information on the primary borrower, which may come from the consumer's application for credit or from employment information that the creditor obtained in approving the account.

The Metro 2 format specifies that base segments be reported for each account submitted. Supplementary segments are reported when relevant to the particular trade line or other data that is furnished.

3.2. Public Record Collection

While the NCRAs rely on a multitude of furnishers to supply creditor trade line information, they also receive public records including bankruptcy records, civil court monetary judgments, and government tax liens from publicly available government sources.

They obtain these records primarily through LexisNexis Risk Data Retrieval Services LLC (LNRDRS). The use of LNRDRS followed the NCRAs' decisions to move from direct collection from hundreds of sources and suppliers to a single data retrieval vendor.

The NCRAs report they do not use criminal records in their credit reports. Rather, the NCRAs utilize public records representing derogatory items in their credit files. Derogatory is defined as negative information that will likely hurt a consumer's credit (e.g., late payments, collection accounts, foreclosures, civil judgments).[41] While each NCRA has its own criteria, public records are generally removed from credit reports once the reportable event becomes obsolete (between seven and ten years depending on the type of information and the applicable statute of limitations).

3.2.1. LNRDRS Data Retrieval

LNRDRS retrieves and sends to each of the three NCRAs between 10 and 20 million public record events per year (roughly one third of which are bankruptcies, tax liens, and civil monetary judgments respectively).[42] All bankruptcy records are pulled electronically from the PACER system, an electronic public access service that allows users to obtain case and docket information from federal appellate, district and bankruptcy courts. Monetary judgments and tax liens are obtained from 10,000 to 12,000 state and local courts and county and state government offices. LNRDRS reports it obtains information on 30% of judgments and liens electronically. For the remaining 70%, LNRDRS deploys a network of independent contractors who manually access public records at government sources and type the local records into a proprietary software system, which screens for duplicates and minimizes typographical errors. A single record collector can typically record approximately 200 events in a day.

In retrieving records for the NCRAs, LNRDRS provides the data in its "raw" form. The NCRAs undertake the responsibility of assigning records to particular consumer files, and adjusting matching criteria for possible errors. Assignment of a court record to a particular consumer can be challenging for the NCRAs because, according to one estimate, SSNs appear on court records only 3% of the time.

4. Furnisher and Data Screening

The NCRAs employ a number of methods to screen furnishers and incoming information for inaccuracies and anomalies. This section examines the vetting and approving of furnishers and various quality screens performed on data files received from furnishers. These methods focus on identifying formatting errors, logical errors, internal inconsistencies, and anomalies.

4.1. New Furnisher Screening

The NCRAs' data quality processes start with their screening of new furnishers.

The NCRAs report that a prospective furnisher can initiate a relationship with them by sending a letter of intent to furnish. Due to the resource and economic costs associated with adding a furnisher, the NCRAs will generally require prospective furnishers to report a minimum of 100 to 200 active accounts per month.[43] Each NCRA reportedly puts prospective furnishers through an initial security screening. Screening generally includes an inspection of features of each business such as its physical headquarters, phone number, website, and business license, as well as company records such as annual reports. Individual NCRAs also may hire third-party investigation services to screen for illegal or unethical business history. Sole proprietorships and new businesses (e.g., in business less than a year) may receive more specialized screening. An NCRA may require the furnishers to submit test files which it will examine to make sure they are Metro 2 compatible. Approved furnishers are trained on Metro 2.

After these initial inspections, NCRA policies may trigger reinspections after risk events such as consumer complaints, suspicious trade lines, variations in data submissions, odd anomalies, and changes in company ownership. At least one NCRA has policies to reinspect new furnishers six months after they start submitting data to assess for data quality and fraud risk.

The NCRAs report that they continue to monitor for data quality and fraud once a furnisher starts contributing live trade line data. One example of furnisher fraud is when a supposed credit repair organization represents itself as a furnisher and attempts to boost the credit scores of consumers with bad credit by reporting fictitious trade lines that the consumers purportedly used and paid back on time.

Overall, the objective of furnisher screening is to reduce the risk of fraud or of poor data quality by screening out furnishers whose systems are not able to report accurate data on customers or report it in the Metro 2 format.

4.2. Checking Furnished Data

Having passed this initial screening, furnishers can start providing data. Furnishers generally provide monthly trade line updates through data file transfers that conform to the Metro or Metro 2 format and contain trade line updates on all of the furnishers' active accounts. All new furnishers are being added under the Metro 2 format, which was first introduced in 1997. Data submitted by a furnisher to an NCRA generally goes through a multi-stage process to identify data irregularities.

Typical data quality checks will identify issues such as blank fields or logical inconsistencies in the data – both at the level of the data file and at the individual consumer's trade line. If a furnished account is reported as closed, and then in a subsequent data feed the furnisher reports a new account balance, the NCRA might flag that inconsistency. Other inconsistencies might be account balances higher than the maximum credit line, duplicate instances of information on the same account being furnished, or data patterns inconsistent with the furnisher's historical pattern of transactions. It is not uncommon for furnishers' bulk files to be initially rejected by the NCRAs.[44] The NCRAs report that furnishers tend to correct most of the problems causing the file rejection, leaving only a small percentage of files permanently rejected. Some data rejections might not result from an error in the data but from format incompatibility when the furnisher uses the wrong codes to update accounts, or the furnished data shows unfamiliar formats because of system changes at the furnisher.

Within file submissions, individual consumer base records and tradeline updates are similarly screened for formatting errors, logical errors, internal inconsistencies, and anomalies. The rejection rates for incoming trade line data from furnishers appear to vary across multiple dimensions (e.g., by individual furnisher, by furnishing industry, by the NCRA receiving the data). For example, submissions from collections agencies tend to have a higher rejection rate than rejections for credit card trade lines.[45]

While the NCRAs' data screens do find errors by identifying anomalies and inconsistencies, these checks rely on underlying furnisher data to be valid. The NCRAs do not conduct independent checks or audits to determine if the data is accurate, such as contacting a consumer to ask if she is properly associated with an account or if the balance reported on an account is true, or checking the record-keeping practices of a furnisher. The NCRAs generally rely on furnishers to report information on consumers that is complete and accurate.

4.3. The Furnisher Rule

In 2009, the Federal Trade Commission, the Federal Reserve Board, the Federal Deposit Insurance Corporation, the National Credit Union Administration, the Office of the Comptroller of the Currency, and the Office of Thrift Supervision issued a joint rule ("Furnisher Rule") implementing the accuracy and integrity and direct dispute provisions for furnishers mandated by the Fair and Accurate Credit Transactions Act (FACTA).[46] The CFPB has since restated this rule.[47]

As a result of FACTA and the Furnisher Rule, furnishers have enhanced obligations to supply accurate data. Each furnisher is required to "establish and implement reasonable written policies and procedures concerning the accuracy and integrity of the information it furnishes to consumer reporting agencies."[48] The procedures should address "deleting, updating, and correcting information in the furnisher's records, as appropriate, to avoid furnishing inaccurate information."[49] The procedures must be appropriate to the "nature, size, complexity, and scope of each furnisher's activities."[50] Appropriate procedures include using standard data reporting formats, maintaining records for a reasonable period of time, providing appropriate oversight of service providers (e.g., companies that provide core processing systems or software used for recordkeeping and account management), furnishing information in a way that prevents re-aging,[*] duplicative reporting, association of information with the wrong consumer, and providing sufficient identifying information about consumers.[51]

5. Compiling Credit Files: "Matching"

Once the NCRAs have received trade line information from a furnisher they must assign it to a specific consumer's identity. Each of the NCRAs has over 200 million active files on individual consumers which are non-duplicative within the particular NCRA.[52] The average credit file contains 13 past and current credit obligations, including nine bank and retail cards and four installment loans (e.g., auto loans, mortgage loans, student loans).[53] In a typical month, an NCRA receives updates on over 1.3 billion trade lines.[54] With this much information included in and added to their databases, the NCRAs face technical and operational challenges in attributing information to the proper consumer's file.

5.1. Identifying the Correct Consumer

To locate and identify a consumer, NCRAs will use various combinations of personal identifying information such as name, address, phone number, date

[*] Re-aging in this context refers to erroneously extending the reporting period of derogatory consumer information by creating a new, later start date when the derogatory event occurred, thus pushing back the clock for removing the derogatory item from the credit report.

of birth, address, and SSN. A given trade line reported by a furnisher may not contain all of this identifying information. Typically, the furnisher reports the personally identifying information that was provided by the consumer in the consumer's original application for credit or through updates (such as for current address or married name) that a consumer may provide in the course of his or her relationship with the furnisher.

The fact that many consumers have the same or similar personal identifiers presents further challenges when a credit bureau tries to match an incoming trade line with the correct consumer's file. In the United States, according to 2000 census figures (the most recent to have last name statistics available), there are more than 2.3 million Americans with the last name of Smith, 1.8 million Americans with the last name of Johnson, 1 million Americans with the last name of Davis, 850 thousand Americans with the last name of Garcia, and 600 thousand Americans with the last name of Lee.[55] As one example, consider the matching challenges posed by relatives with same first and last name, but different middle names, who reside at the same address, and who do not regularly use their middle name when applying for credit.

Adding to the complexity, millions of individuals change how they identify themselves over time or between furnishers. Each year, a sizeable number of Americans change their name through marriage and divorce. Separately, consumers do not necessarily refer to themselves consistently in credit applications. For example, a woman named Elizabeth may use her full name on one application and then refer to herself with a nickname "Betty," "Beth," "Liz," or "Eliza" on another credit transaction. Finally, creditor practices may vary as to the personally identifying information they require in their loan or credit applications, with the result that the criteria one creditor uses to identify a consumer in a trade line update may vary from how another creditor identifies him or her.

5.2. Posting and Organizing Account Information in Consumer Files

Once a trade line has passed the NCRAs' initial vetting and screening, the NCRAs assign or post that trade line to the credit file of a specific consumer if they believe there is a match. As discussed below, inaccuracies may result from this process.

The manner in which each NCRA posts incoming data to a consumer's file, and the way its files are organized, depends on the particular structure of its database, or its unique "data architecture." The NCRAs take two different approaches to organizing personal data in their data networks: (1) flat file system and (2) "PINning" technology.

5.2.1. Flat File Systems

At least one NCRA organizes its database like a traditional flat filing system so that each consumer is linked to one file.[56] Consumers' files are distinguished through matching logic using a consumer's personal identifiers such as name, address, SSN, and date of birth. Multiple or fragmented files can occur for a single person when information is reported with different identifying information such as a different last name. Fragmented files on the same consumer will remain distinct until the NCRA receives new information about the fragments (e.g., a unifying name, address, phone number) that indicates they should be combined. In some cases, matching algorithms will assign the trade line to a file that, according to the algorithm, represents the best match even when all of the identifiers do not match up perfectly, or when only a limited number of identifiers are contained with the trade line.

5.2.2. PINning Technology

Another method uses a unique personal identification number (PIN) to organize consumer files.[57] Instead of having a single file for each consumer, it uses the consumer's assigned PIN to link information on the consumer from multiple databases including inquiry, trade line, employment, public record, and address databases. Each furnished trade line data element, inquiry, or public record is entered into the network with an associated PIN in a relational database. PINs are assigned to trade lines based on algorithms that find the consumer that best matches the personal (header) information accompanying the trade line. When a consumer report is requested by a creditor or a consumer requests a credit report, the NCRA assembles the consumer report in real-time using the PIN as the central link to the different databases.

In this system, matching algorithms are used to assign a new incoming trade line or public record to the PIN that represents the best possible fit based on the personally identifying information associated with the trade line.

The CFPB has no data on the relative accuracy of flat-file vs. PIN-based architectures.

6. Inaccuracies in Credit Files and Credit Reports

Given the volume of data handled, the challenges of matching tradelines to the correct consumer files, and the number and variety of furnishers, inaccuracies in some credit files inevitably occur. Inaccuracies in credit files and credit reports can occur where information that does not belong to a consumer is attached to his or her file, where information belonging to a consumer is omitted from the file, or where there are factual inaccuracies in trade line or other information in the consumer's file. Some of these inaccuracies can be attributed to matching challenges in assigning a trade line to a consumer's file. Other causes of inaccuracies include data and data entry errors, NCRA system or process inaccuracies, furnisher system or process inaccuracies, identity fraud, or time lags.

6.1. Types of Inaccuracies in Credit Files and Reports

The following are among the types of inaccuracies that appear in credit files and the reports derived from them.

- **Inclusion of accounts or records in a credit file that do not belong to the consumer, commonly called a mixed file:** Credit reports can contain trade lines or public records about a consumer other than the one who is the subject of the credit report.
- **Omission of accounts or records belonging to the consumer**: A credit account or public record that belongs to the consumer's file can be erroneously placed in another consumer's file, leading to a mixed file, as described above.[58] Alternatively, credit bureau matching algorithms or gaps in data can lead to a consumer trade line being kept separate from the rest of the consumer's file.
- **Trade line or record inaccurately represents information pertaining to the consumer's account with the creditor**: A credit file can inaccurately depict the terms and status of a valid account such as inaccurately depicting the date an account was closed, the credit limit for the account, or whether a trade line is delinquent. Similarly, a collection item on the report may inaccurately reflect the payment status of the debt or the amount of money owed.

  It is worth noting that in some cases consumers are mistaken about the presence of inaccuracies in their account. For example, a consumer may believe he or she paid a bill when it was not paid. A consumer may believe that paying an item in collection removes the collection history from one's credit report, which it does not. A consumer may believe he or she paid an account on time, when under the terms of the account, it was late. Or a consumer may simply not recognize a trade line even though it is legitimate.

6.2. Causes of Credit File Inaccuracies

The inaccuracies identified in Section 6.1 can come from a variety of causes.

- **Data and data entry errors**: Furnishers can input accurate consumer information incorrectly or make typographical mistakes (e.g., transposing two digits in an SSN, misspelling names, transposing first and middle names).[59] Consumers (when applying for a loan) can provide inaccurate data to furnishers. For both of these types of inaccuracies, the credit bureau could pass along the inaccuracy to the consumer's file.
  Data errors can also lead to file matching problems by causing the bureau to put the trade line into a separate or "orphan" file distinct from the consumer's original credit file, and thus not include it in the consumer's credit report. Alternatively, data inaccuracy could cause a consumer's trade line to be mixed in with another consumer's file (e.g., when the mistake causes the consumer's header information to match or resemble the identity of another consumer).
- **Bureau file matching inaccuracies**: Inaccuracies can occur when a bureau assigns a trade line to a consumer's file or when it determines the credit file that matches the consumer named in a creditor inquiry. A matching error can occur for a variety of reasons.
  - Matching errors may result from creditor inquiries and trade lines that contain a limited set of identifiers relating to the consumer. For example, a lender inquiry may omit information such as date of birth or SSN.
  - Family members with similar identity information such as fathers and sons with common names (e.g., Jr., Sr.) can experience commingling of files, especially if they reside at the same addresses and distinguishing information is not provided.

- Unrelated individuals with similar names and identity information get linked together because a name or SSN is incorrectly inputted.

In some cases, when a consumer changes personal information (e.g., his or her name) the bureau will be unable to match the new trade line to an existing file until the bureau has confidence that the new information belongs to the existing consumer. A common example occurs when a consumer changes names after getting married or divorced.

Until the bureau can link the individual pre- and post- name change, that individual's information might reside in two different files.

- **Bureau process errors**: An example of a process error would be if a credit bureau failed to prevent the reappearance in a consumer's credit report of inaccurate data that was removed as a result of a consumer dispute reinvestigation. Such errors can occur despite the bureau maintaining procedures to permanently remove or suppress identified inaccuracies as required by the FCRA.[60]
- **Identity fraud/theft**: Identity thieves can compromise a consumer's credit history by creating new credit, utility, or health care accounts in the consumer's name and then letting them go unpaid. As these accounts go delinquent and are pushed to collections, the consumer victim's credit rating can plummet. Fraudsters may also take over existing consumer accounts, often disguising the account theft by changing the billing address of the applicant with the lending institution, or making purchases over the Internet. Additionally, fraudsters can create synthetic identities using an innocent consumer's SSN or other identifiers like last name and birthdate.[61]
- **Furnisher system or process inaccuracies**: Inaccuracies can occur because of limitations in the processes furnishers and public records providers use in handling consumer transactions. Examples include:
  - Attributing ownership to an account on which an individual is only an authorized user;
  - Failing to post a payment;
  - Assigning a payment to the wrong account;
  - Failing to update records (e.g., tax liens or other judgments that are still listed as open even though they have been paid or resolved);
  - Failing to permanently change records when a consumer successfully disputes an inaccuracy, with the result that faulty information is re-reported;

- Listing closed accounts as open;
- Reporting an incorrect credit limit; and
- Transfering loans from one owner or servicer to another owner or servicer with different record-keeping systems can result in lost data or lost payment records.

Furnishers and consumers can disagree on the status of credit accounts (e.g., whether a payment was late). These disagreements can be addressed, if not always resolved, through the dispute processes that consumers have the right to initiate under the Fair Credit Billing Act (e.g., for billing disputes involving credit cards, department store accounts, other open-end credit accounts)[62] or the FCRA.

Additionally, certain trade lines may be reported by multiple furnishers over time. Examples include trade lines reported by a debt buyer that were previously reported by a creditor from whom the debt buyer acquired the accounts, or mortgage loans for which the servicing rights were sold from one servicer to another. In these cases, the bureaus not only match the trade line with the correct consumer's file, but may also determine when the incoming trade line reflects the continuation of a previously reported trade line in the consumer's file. To facilitate correct depiction of such trade lines over time, the Metro 2 policy is for furnishers who are new account owners to list the name of the original creditor in file updates. Omission of this information by a furnisher who has bought the debt, and/or failure by account sellers to acknowledge when accounts have been sold, may result in duplicate trade lines in a consumer file.

- **Time lags**: Differences can occur due to time lags between a consumer transaction and its reporting to a credit bureau file (e.g., paying a past due bill or opening a new account). Time lags are a significant issue in the updating of public records. According to one industry source, it takes some state courts, on average, two months to transcribe a court judgment into a written court decision.[63]

6.3. Consumer Impact of Inaccuracies

Each of these types of credit report errors may affect how a creditor or a credit score assesses the credit worthiness of a consumer. Trade line errors can both hurt or help a consumer's credit score. An omitted current trade line, for example, may lower a credit score. Likewise, a credit score may be unfairly reduced by a negative trade line that belongs to another consumer, or by duplicate trade lines that are treated as two separate credit relationships. On the other hand, if a delinquent trade line was inadvertently assigned to another consumer's file or if a furnisher incorrectly marked a delinquent trade line as current, the error could help the consumer's score.

7. Disputing Credit Report Errors

Recognizing the possibility of inaccuracies, the FCRA gives consumers the right to dispute information they deem inaccurate with an NCRA, a furnisher (in cases covered by the Furnisher Rule), or both. The FCRA requires NCRAs and furnishers to "reinvestigate" information contained in a consumer's credit file when the consumer disputes its accuracy.[64] Further, the statute gives consumers several mechanisms for obtaining the information contained in their credit files in order to review them for possible inaccuracies. Consumers can get a free credit report, that is, obtain a file disclosure for free, (i) once every 12 months from the NCRAs and nationwide specialty consumer reporting agencies,[65] (ii) in connection with risk-based pricing and adverse action notices,[66] (iii) if they are unemployed and intend to apply for employment within 60 days,[67] (iv) if they are recipients of welfare assistance,[68] (v) if they have reason to believe their credit file is inaccurate due to fraud,[69] (vi) in connection with requested initial or extended fraud alerts,[70] or (vii) if permitted by state law. Consumers can also review their credit files by purchasing them directly or when they receive their credit files as part of a paid credit monitoring service subscription. Consumers sometimes also receive information from reports or copies of reports from a user such as a bank, mortgage broker, or landlord.

The CFPB estimates that as many as 44 million consumers obtained copies of their consumer file disclosure annually in 2010 and 2011 – either as a result of obtaining free annual file disclosures through annualcreditreport.com (15.9 million);[71] through one of many various credit monitoring services (26 million);[72] obtaining disclosures directly from the NCRAs after receiving adverse action notices or risk- based pricing notices (approximately 1 million);[73] or from lenders directly or through fraud alerts, requests based on unemployment or welfare status, and where free under state law (approximately 0.5 million for this catch-all category).[74]

In 2011, the NCRAs received approximately 8 million consumer contacts disputing the completeness or accuracy of one or more trade lines, public records, or credit header information (identification information) in their files.[75] [*] Based on these contacts, the number of credit-active consumers who disputed one or more items with an NCRA in 2011 ranges from 1.3% to 3.9%. On average across the NCRAs, consumers filed 42% of their disputes online, 44% by mail, and 13% by phone. The remainder of consumers communicated their disputes by fax, walk-ins, or other methods.[76] Many of these consumers disputed information about more than one tradeline or other item in their file, leading to approximately 32 to 38 million dispute reinvestigations.[77] This volume has declined significantly since 2007 when consumers were more active in applying for credit, particularly in the mortgage market. In 2007, a high volume year, the NCRAs received disputes on 47 to 53 million items.[78]

The number of consumer dispute requests (8 million) appears high relative to the total number of consumers who see their credit files (44 million). However, the CFPB is unable to estimate a dispute rate for consumers who see their files for several reasons. First, no data is available on the overlap of disputes by consumers among the three largest NCRAs. Thus the range of unique consumers who filed complaints could be up to 8 million or substantially less if high volumes of consumers filed complaints with multiple NCRAs. Second, it is unclear how many consumers obtained copies of their credit reports or file disclosures by more than one means in a given year. Additionally, an unknown number of consumers may initiate disputes without their reports after being advised by lenders of specific negative items appearing on their reports.

7.1. Credit Bureau and Furnisher Disputes

Consumers can elect to dispute the completeness or accuracy of their credit file through the NCRA or other bureau that provided their report, directly with the furnisher who provided the disputed trade line (in cases covered by the Furnisher Rule), or both. The nature and timeframes for responses to disputes are specified in the FCRA.

Under Section 611 of the FCRA, if a consumer disputes the completeness or accuracy of his or her credit file, the credit bureau has an obligation to conduct a reasonable reinvestigation.[79] The bureau must generally complete a reinvestigation within 30 days, in which it must consider all the relevant

[*] This estimate counts contacts made by a single consumer to multiple NCRAs as multiple contacts.

information supplied by the consumer.[80] Moreover, it has five business days to forward the dispute to the relevant furnisher.[81] The credit bureau notification to the furnisher shall include all relevant information received from the consumer.[82] If the reinvestigation determines that the consumer's data is inaccurate, incomplete, or cannot be verified, the bureau must delete the disputed data.[83] Furnishers have independent obligations under the FCRA, after receiving notice from a CRA of a consumer dispute, pursuant to Section 611 to conduct an investigation into the disputed information, to review all the relevant information provided by the CRA, and to report the results of the investigation to the CRA.[84]

As stated above, consumers can also dispute the accuracy of information directly with the furnisher of the information. Under the Furnisher Rule, a furnisher must conduct a reasonable investigation of a consumer's dispute about his or her liability for a debt to the furnisher, the terms of the debt, the consumer's performance concerning the account at issue, or "other information contained in a consumer report regarding an account or relationship with the furnisher that bears on the consumer's credit worthiness, credit standing," or other credit reporting factors.[85] The furnisher also must "review all relevant information provided by the consumer" and complete an investigation and report the results back to the consumer in the same time frame as if the dispute was sent to a consumer reporting agency.[86] If the investigation finds furnished information was inaccurate, the furnisher must promptly notify each CRA that received the information of its determination and provide corrected information.[87]

7.2. Trade Line Dispute Rates

The NCRAs see variations in dispute rate by furnisher, account status, and industry. The dispute rates for the active trade lines among the 100 largest furnishers generally fall within a range between 0.05% and 2.0%.[88] The dispute rate reported by the NCRAs on delinquent trade lines not yet in collections is approximately 1.1%.[89] Dispute rates for specific industries vary widely as well. Some of this variation may be due to variations in data quality controls at individual furnishers. Other differences may simply be due to the fact that some trade lines and industries, by their nature, are likely to generate more disputes from consumers than others. One would expect, for example, that consumers would be more likely to challenge trade lines with reported delinquencies or collections actions than trade lines that only reflect positive information. Likewise, one would expect higher dispute rates in credit categories where delinquency rates are high (e.g., on subprime loans as opposed to prime loans).

Figure 3 describes the average trade line dispute rates for different types of furnishers.[90]

Collection trade lines generate significantly higher numbers of consumer disputes than other types of trade lines – four times higher than auto and five times higher than mortgage dispute rates. Collections and delinquent trade lines also reflect a disproportionate percentage of all accuracy disputes by consumers with the NCRAs. Almost 40% of all consumer disputes at the NCRAs, on average, can be linked to collections.[92]

Multiple factors likely converge to generate a high volume of collections item disputes. First, in contrast to other types of trade lines, 100% of collections trade lines correspond to negative information on a consumer's credit record. Consumers have a greater incentive to dispute information in a credit file that harms their credit record than information that favorably reflects their ability and willingness to pay back a loan.

Both the discontinuous nature of consumers' relationships with debt collectors (the collector has limited interest in a long-term relationship with the consumer) and the collections industry's data management practices also may contribute to increased disputes.[93] Collections debt can be placed with third-party collection agencies or sold to debt buyers multiple times. With each assignment or sale there are risks of account data being compromised or lost, and with multiple transfers, the risk of errors may increase. Debt buyers and debt collectors may lack the original documentation (e.g., consumer applications, statement showing last payment made, charge-off statement) underlying a debt, contributing to mistakes. Additionally, other than the sale of mortgages, consumers generally are not required to be notified when debt is sold or assigned to a collection agency, so they may not associate the entity reporting negative trade line information with the name of the original creditor account.[94] While the industry's standard Metro 2 data furnishing format has a field for debt collectors to report the originating creditor associated with the debt, collectors may not always report the field. Separately, some consumers may knowingly (or with the encouragement of certain credit repair organizations) dispute valid collection items or judgments in the hopes of removing them from their credit files and increasing their credit scores.

Below, Figure 4 contains the average dispute rates of the top 100 furnishers to two NCRAs in 2011 by furnisher size.

Industry Type	Disputes/Year per Active Trade Line
Bank Card and Retail Card	0.17%
Finance Companies[91]	0.19%
Mortgage	0.21%
Auto	0.27%
Student Loans	0.29%
Collection/Debt Buyers	1.06%

Figure 3. Dispute Rates by Industry Type.

Furnisher Size	Average Percent of Trade Lines Disputed per Year
Top 10	0.20%
Top 11-25	0.26%
26-50	0.35%
51-100	0.47%

Source: Industry statistics.

Figure 4. Trade Line Dispute Rates by Furnisher Size.

As indicated earlier, the Top 10 furnishers provide a majority of each of the NCRAs' trade lines. These furnishers are multi-line banks and financial services providers with high proportions of prime borrowers. Higher dispute rates among the smaller furnishers (ranked by the number of trade lines each furnisher reports) may reflect that more of them are collection agencies (a fragmented industry including many small firms) or have proportionately larger subprime lending portfolios (accounts that are more likely to be delinquent and to generate consumer disputes).*

At present, the NCRAs do not appear to regularly measure dispute rates of furnished trade lines at the industry or individual furnisher level and they do not all measure dispute rates in a consistent fashion.

* It should be possible to identify furnishers who are disproportionately responsible for tradeline disputes relative to furnishers of similar type and size. For example, using a common measure of disputes per 1000 trade lines reported, a credit card issuer's dispute rate could be compared to the average dispute rate for credit card issuers, and an overall dispersion of dispute rates. Furnishers who are outliers (i.e. have high dispute rates) in industries that have a high dispute rate dispersion among furnishers may be appropriate targets for a process review that may yield sources of reporting inaccuracies, data omissions, or billing errors that result in a high level of credit bureau disputes. Helping to identify and address these furnishers' root causes of disputes might yield a reduction in disputes and improvements in credit file accuracy.

7.3. Resolving Trade Line Disputes: The e-OSCAR System

The NCRAs handle most consumers' trade line disputes they receive through an electronic information network called e-OSCAR (the Online Solution for Complete and Accurate Reporting). The e-OSCAR network began in 1993 as a system run by the Associated Credit Bureaus, now the CDIA. Four companies built and still own e-OSCAR – Equifax, Experian, Innovis, and TransUnion. The current Internet-based system was created in 2001; the CDIA created the Online Data Exchange (OLDE) in 2006 to independently operate the system. In 2011, 16,000 furnishers connected to these companies through e-OSCAR.[95]

In the last three months of 2011, 33% of e-OSCAR disputes related to claims by a consumer that an account in their file did not belong to them, either because of error or identity theft. In another 15% of disputes, consumers claimed the information on a trade line was inaccurate. About 4% of consumer disputes involved the reporting of a consumer's current account balance, and another 4% of disputes involved collections items about which consumers claimed not to be aware.[96]

7.3.1. The Dispute Process

According to the NCRAs, trade line disputes handled by them pass through five steps.

1. **Consumer initiates a dispute and reason codes are assigned**: The process starts with a dispute by a consumer to one of the NCRAs. Consumers can initiate a dispute online, by phone, by mail, by fax, or in person. When a consumer initiates the dispute online the consumer may provide a narrative description of the nature of the dispute and why the consumer believes the information contained in the credit report to be in error. The consumer must also select one or two reason codes from a list of 29 different codes that characterize the nature of the dispute.[97] In mail and phone disputes, NCRA representatives will assign the dispute codes they deem appropriate and may occasionally supplement the dispute code with a narrative statement.
2. **NCRA internally reviews dispute**: The NCRA then investigates the dispute request using proprietary decision rules to see if it can resolve the dispute internally without having to forward the dispute to the furnisher. For example, the NCRAs will internally resolve disputes they consider frivolous such as resubmitted but previously resolved

disputes where no new information is provided.* Separately, an NCRA may resolve a dispute in a consumer's favor under certain circumstances, such as if the documentation provided by the consumer "can be reasonably verified as authentic."[98] Disputes over the consumer's identifying information (e.g., name, address, SSN) also tend to be resolved internally. In such cases, an NCRA may simply adopt the consumer's correction or use internal or external identity verification tools to evaluate the consumer's claim. The NCRAs resolved or rejected an average of 15% of the disputes they received in 2011.[99] The CFPB does not know what percentage of these resolutions was in the consumer's favor.

3. **Dispute sent to furnisher**: If the dispute cannot be resolved internally, the NCRA will forward the dispute through e-OSCAR to the appropriate furnisher with dispute codes through an electronic form called automated consumer dispute verification (ACDV). Supplementing the dispute code(s), the ACDV can provide up to 255 characters of consumer-supplied text describing the dispute in a free-form text field. In 2011, free-form text was added, on average, to 26% of the NCRAs' e-OSCAR transmission, although the percentage varies from NCRA to NCRA based, in part, on whether the online form contains a text field. Consumers can provide supplementary documentation (such as billing or other records or letters to and from creditors) regarding a dispute via mail to an NCRA, but it appears the NCRAs generally do not pass these documents along to furnishers.
4. **Furnisher investigates and responds**: The data furnisher investigates the ACDV request and routes back the response through e-OSCAR to the requesting NCRA. This typically involves a furnisher representative reviewing the furnisher's electronic records of the disputed account and then selecting a response that reflects what the furnisher's records have shown. In e-OSCAR, furnishers can make four different types of responses: (a) verify account as accurate, (b) modify account/trade line information as indicated, (c) delete account, or (d) delete account due to fraud.

* One NCRA reported that approximately 16% of disputes do not result in an e-OSCAR transaction because the consumer had previously submitted an identical dispute and the NCRA had recently forwarded the dispute to the furnisher, who had investigated and verified the data.

The CDIA reports that in a recent 120 day period in 2012, 22% of furnisher responses indicated that the initial data was accurate (rejecting the consumer's claim), 61% modified a trade line or other piece of information, 13% deleted a trade line or other piece of information, and 0.5% deleted a trade line or other piece of information due to fraud. The NCRAs deleted or modified, as indicated by the consumer, 4% of disputed trade lines because the furnisher did not provide a response within the statutory time frame.[100] The high percentage of furnishers who modify disputed data should be qualified by noting that many larger furnishers will automatically update a trade line with the latest account information (e.g., a new balance) upon receiving a dispute, regardless of whether the furnisher deemed reported information to be inaccurate; thus, a modification may not necessarily reflect concurrence with the consumer's dispute.[101]

As revealed in Figure 5 below, these figures are similar to those reported by the CDIA to the FTC and the Federal Reserve Board for the first five months of 2004 in those agencies' 2006 study on the FCRA dispute process and in GAO testimony to Congress in 2003.[102] The most significant change has been that the percentage of trade lines that were deleted as a result of furnishers not responding to disputes within 30 days has dropped from 16% in 2002 to 4% in 2011.

5. **Referral:** If an account is modified or deleted, the furnisher is supposed to send copies of its modification to each CRA with whom the data furnisher has a reporting relationship. This way all the NCRAs can meet their responsibilities to update the consumer's credit files, where applicable.

The CFPB has been unable to estimate the volume of disputes filed directly with furnishers. To date, the NCRAs report little impact from the Furnisher Rule on their volumes of consumer disputes.[103]

7.3.2. Limitations of the e-OSCAR Process

Consumer advocates have raised compliance concerns with respect to the adequacy or completeness of these transmissions to furnishers, which are principally dispute codes along with supplementary text added in a minority of cases. The FCRA requires NCRAs to send the data furnisher a notice that includes "*all relevant information regarding the dispute that the agency has received from the consumer*."[104] The NCRAs argue that most disputes can be fairly and completely summarized using the e-OSCAR numeric codes. The e-OSCAR system currently does not permit documents provided by consumers, such as statements or letters from creditors, to be forwarded to furnishers as attachments. Industry sources cited technological limitations, challenges evaluating the authenticity of consumer documents, and privacy concerns as impediments to adding such attachments.

Consumer advocates further argue the NCRAs have a systemic bias that defers to furnishers' records in determining whether or not disputed information is accurate.[105] They note that if a furnisher verifies previously reported information as accurate, the NCRAs will generally accord such a response greater weight than the consumer's claims that the information is inaccurate. Likewise, when the furnisher responds that the account should be modified, deleted, or deleted due to fraud, the NCRAs generally implement these responses as received. The advocates argue that NCRAs do not independently validate information contained in furnishers' records.

However, the NCRAs have had occasion to adopt policies to suppress information that is subject to high levels of disputes. For instance, one NCRA developed special policies to address problems with certain disputes about small dollar collection items.

7.4. Public Record Disputes

Consumers' disputes regarding the accuracy of public records in their personal credit files are not investigated through the e-OSCAR system. The NCRAs initiate their investigation of a public record dispute by again collecting the public record directly from the government source or, at their election, contracting for LNRDRS to conduct this re-checking of the record. LNRDRS collects a combined 1-2 million public records annually at the NCRAs' request.[*]

When forwarding a dispute verification query to LNRDRS, the NCRAs provide the company one of up to 24 reason codes explaining the consumer dispute. In about 60 to 70% of the requests that LNRDRS receives from the NCRAs for verification, the consumer asserts that the public record is not his/hers. In another 20 to 25% of the disputes, a consumer asserts that he or she has paid the judgment or lien.[106]

---

[*] It is not known how many consumers generate these 1-2 million public record reviews as the average number of disputes per consumer file is unknown. It is also possible that consumers dispute the same public record with multiple NCRAs.

Result	Percent of Disputes		
	2011 (120 Day Period)	2004 (First 5 months)	2002 (First 3 quarters)
Data modified per furnisher's instructions	61%	54%	27%
Information verified as reported	22%	22%	46%
Data deleted per data furnisher's request	13%	18%	10.5%
Data deleted due to no furnisher response	4%	6%	16%
Trade line removed due to fraud	0.5%		

Sources: For 2011: Stuart Pratt, President, CDIA; For 2004: The Federal Trade Commission and the Board of Governors of the Federal Reserve System, *Report to Congress on the Fair Credit Reporting Act Dispute Process*; For 2002: Richard Hillman, GAO-03-1036T.

Figure 5. Dispute results.

In response to a dispute verification query related to the status of a public record, LNRDRS will typically send a data collector to the public record source to re-check the record and look for updates. LNRDRS will then report one of three statuses back to the NCRA: (1) status has changed (e.g., lien paid off); (2) status is unchanged (e.g., current record remains most accurate); or (3) unable to verify. LNRDRS does not verify the content of the underlying public record as accurate or determine if an NCRA appropriately linked the record to a consumer. In the case of public records, the NCRAs retain responsibility for determining whether a public record should or should or not be attached to a consumer's file.

According to LNRDRS, it performs public record re-checks at the request of the NCRAs, typically within five business days. LNRDRS reports that in 99.5% of all dispute verification queries it handles on behalf of the NCRAs, it is able to locate the record at issue, re-check it, and respond to the request. Time lags are a factor in many public record complaints as it reportedly can take, on average in some state courts, two months between the time of a judgment and its transcription into a public record.[107]

8. Monitoring and Measuring Credit Reporting Accuracy

In consideration of the importance of data accuracy to consumers and to decision makers using credit reports, there have been several recent initiatives to measure credit report accuracy.

8.1. The FTC's National Study of Credit Report Accuracy

The FTC is expected soon to complete a decade-long study on credit report accuracy that the agency was mandated to undertake in FACTA. At the end of 2012, the FTC expects to issue its fifth interim report of its "National Study of Credit Report Accuracy." The FTC expects to issue a final report in 2014. It will attempt to estimate the proportion of credit files that contain material errors, identify the main types of errors and their frequency, as well as their impact on consumers' credit scores and hence the errors' impacts on affected consumers' access to and cost of credit. To accomplish this, the study has recruited 1,000 consumer participants randomly selected from across the country who have reviewed their reports from the NCRAs with experts who help them understand their report, identify errors, and distinguish material from non-material errors (in terms of potential impact on the consumers' credit scores). Identified errors have been submitted to the respective NCRAs as disputes for resolution. Reinvestigation resolution results will be indicative of the overall error rate of trade lines and public records, and the percentage of credit reports containing corrected errors will indicate the overall rate of credit report accuracy. Further, credit reports containing corrections will be re-scored and differences between credit scores pre- and post-correction will provide an indication of the materiality of the credit report errors.

8.2. Industry Research

In May 2011, the Policy & Economic Research Council (PERC) published a report commissioned by the CDIA, which generally followed the FTC's planned methodology, with significant differences in sample selection. Further, compared to the FTC study, the participating consumers in the PERC study were not provided in-person coaching to identify errors. The PERC study found that a sample of 2,338 consumers viewing their credit reports identified potential errors in 19% of credit reports.[108] Of the potential inaccuracies, 37% were about "header" information that would not affect a consumer's credit score.[109] Consumers chose to dispute one or more pieces of trade line information for 7.4% of credit reports.[110] In 45% of the consumer disputes, the consumers' trade lines were modified. In another 41% of the consumer disputes, the disputed trade lines were deleted.[111] The study defined corrections leading to a 25 point or more change in the consumer's VantageScore as a material correction that could shift the consumer's score into a different pricing tier. The resultant CRA corrections in the relevant trade line information resulted in credit score increases of 25 points or more in 0.93% of credit reports examined or 10 points or more in 1.78% of the credit reports examined.[112] Extrapolating to one estimate of the U.S. credit-scoreable population, approximately 3 million Americans would experience score increases of 10 points or more if they reviewed and disputed inaccuracies in their credit reports.[113]

8.3. Consumer Advocate Sponsored Research

A consumer group-sponsored study produced different results. A 2004 survey by the U.S. Public Interest Research Group (PIRG) of its own members concluded "twenty-five percent (25%) of the credit reports surveyed contained serious errors that could result in the denial of credit, such as false delinquencies or accounts that did not belong to the consumer."[114] The results of the survey must be qualified considering the small sample size (154 respondents) and the potential biases in the selection of the respondents (surveys were filled out by PIRG staff, coalition partners, friends and family).[115]

8.4. Future Accuracy Measurement and Related Metrics

Ongoing efforts to measure credit report accuracy will likely continue to rely on consumers to identify potential inaccuracies in their credit reports and to rely on the dispute resolution system to validate that inaccuracies have occurred.

Because information contained in credit files originates from diverse sources such as furnishers, consumers (who respond to lender applications with certain personal information), or public records providers, there is no single source of comprehensive and reliable data regarding the precise identities of consumers or the status of their credit relationships. For this reason, efforts to measure overall credit report accuracy have necessarily involved review of credit reports and individual trade lines by consumers themselves who are most likely to know when information reported about them is correct or incorrect, although consumers may not always interpret their reports correctly.

Further, the consumer dispute process will not identify or ameliorate certain types of errors that may be associated with the NCRA matching processes. For example, it is difficult for consumers to identify when their personal information is diverted to an "orphan" file because consumers wouldn't see such information in a file disclosure. Additionally, trade lines inaccurately associated with a consumer's files due to mismatching of consumers with similar identifying information have high likelihoods of being confirmed as accurate by furnishers.

Finally, to the extent matching processes used to compile credit reports yield different results in reports provided to users from file disclosures provided to consumers (e.g., because lenders and other users may provide more limited consumer-identifying information in their inquiries) it is possible that consumers and users may not always receive the exact same information. On July 20, 2012 the CFPB published its larger participant rule permitting it to supervise companies with annual receipts from "consumer reporting," as defined in the rule, of over $7 million. That rule became effective on September 30, 2012.

In announcing the Bureau's new authorities, Director Richard Cordray indicated that the agency would treat as its initial priorities in examining consumer reporting agencies for compliance with the FCRA and other consumer financial protection laws "accuracy of the information received by the credit reporting companies, their accuracy in assembling and maintaining that information, and the processes that govern error resolution."[*]

The CFPB is also now accepting consumer complaints about credit reporting, giving consumers individual- level complaint assistance for the first time at the federal level with consumer reporting agencies. Finally, as part of its supervision of large financial institutions, it is examining the consumer reporting practices of the furnishers that are responsible for a preponderance of information contained in credit reports.

These efforts will give the CFPB an opportunity to further evaluate the potential roles of credit report accuracy measurements and of metrics related to the NCRAs' and furnishers' various business processes in improving overall accuracy in the U.S. credit reporting system. As appropriate, the CFPB may consider the development and implementation of data quality and accuracy metrics to reduce risk to consumers and assure compliance with FCRA obligations.

---

* http://www.consumerfinance.gov/speeches/prepared-remarks-by-richard-cordray-on-credit-reporting/.

GLOSSARY

CDIA – Consumer Data Industry Association. The CDIA is an international trade association that represents consumer data companies including the nationwide consumer reporting agencies.

Consumer Report – Reports provided by consumer reporting agencies to lenders and other users. The FCRA defines a consumer report as "any written, oral, or other communication of any information by a consumer reporting agency bearing on a consumer's credit worthiness, credit standing, credit capacity, character, general reputation, personal characteristics, or mode of living which is used or expected to be used or collected in whole or in part for the purpose of serving as a factor in establishing the consumer's eligibility for (A) credit or insurance to be used primarily for personal, family, or household purposes; (B) employment purposes; or (C) any other purpose authorized under section 604 [of the FCRA]." The FCRA provides a limited number of exclusions to this definition.

Consumer Reporting Agency – The FCRA defines a consumer reporting agency (CRA) as "any person, which, for monetary fees, dues, or on a cooperative nonprofit basis, regularly engages in whole or in part in the practice of assembling or evaluating consumer credit information or other information on consumers for the purpose of furnishing consumer reports to third parties, and which uses any means or facility of interstate commerce for the purpose of preparing or furnishing consumer reports."

Credit File/Consumer File – The information about a consumer that is contained in the databases of credit reporting agencies. According to the FCRA, the term "file," when used in connection with information on any consumer, means all of the information on that consumer recorded and retained by a consumer reporting agency regardless of how that information is stored.

Consumer File Disclosure – Information provided to a consumer when that consumer requests a copy of the information in his or her file at the NCRA.

Credit Report – Popular term for consumer reports used or purchased by lenders.

Credit Reporting Agency/Credit Bureau – Popular term for consumer reporting agencies in the business of providing consumer reports to lenders.

ECOA – Equal Credit Opportunity Act.

e-OSCAR – The Online Solution for Complete and Accurate Reporting. Web-based computer software system used by Equifax, TransUnion, Experian, and Innovis to communicate with furnishers about consumer disputes.

FCRA – Fair Credit Reporting Act.

Furnisher – Generally refers to an entity that provides information relating to its own transactions or experiences with consumers to one or more consumer reporting agencies for inclusion in consumer reports.

Inquiry – A request for a consumer report.

Metro 2® – The industry standard format for furnisher data contributions created in 1997 by the CDIA on behalf of Equifax, TransUnion, Experian, and Innovis.

NCRA – Nationwide consumer reporting agency. For the purpose of this paper, an NCRA means Equifax, Experian, or TransUnion.

Public Record – Generally, a record that a governmental body is required to maintain, and which must be accessible to scrutiny by the public. Definitions of public records can vary by federal, state, or local jurisdiction.

Reinvestigation – An investigation by a consumer reporting agency or a furnisher into the accuracy or completeness of information in a consumer's credit file in response to a consumer dispute of such information.

Trade Line – Information furnished by a creditor to a consumer reporting agency that reflects the consumer's account status and activity. Trade line information includes the name of companies where the applicant has accounts, dates accounts were opened, credit limits, types of accounts, balances owed and payment histories.

APPENDIX. E-OSCAR DISPUTE CODES

The 29 e-OSCAR dispute codes are as follows:

- Not his/hers
- Belongs to another individual with same/similar name
- Not aware of collection
- Late due to change of address – never received statement
- Settlement or partial payment accepted
- Claims paid the original creditor before collection status or paid before charge-off
- Credit limit and/or high credit amount incorrect
- Included in the bankruptcy of another person
- Claims account closed
- Claims account closed by consumer
- Contract cancelled or rescinded
- Account included in bankruptcy
- Claims active military duty
- Insurance claim delayed
- Account involved litigation
- Claims victim of natural or declared disaster
- Claims account deferred
- Not liable for account (i.e. ex-spouse, business)
- Account reaffirmed or not included in bankruptcy
- Claims true identity fraud, account fraudulently opened
- Claims account take-over, fraudulent charges made on account
- Disputes dates of last payment/date opened/date of first delinquency/date closed
- Disputes present/previous account status/payment history profile/payment rating
- Disputes special comment/compliance condition code/narrative remarks
- Disputes account type or terms duration/terms frequency or portfolio type disputed
- Disputes current balance
- Claims company will change

- Claims company will delete
- Consumer states inaccurate information

End Notes

[1] See, e.g., 15 USC 1681e(b) (requiring consumer reporting agencies to "follow reasonable procedures to assure maximum possible accuracy of the information concerning an individual about whom the report relates"); 15 USC 1681i (requiring a consumer reporting agency to reinvestigate upon receiving a consumer dispute); 15 USC 1681s-2(a)(1)(A) (prohibiting a furnisher from furnishing information that it "knows or has reasonable cause to believe that the information is inaccurate"); 15 USC 1681s-2(a)(1)(B) (prohibiting the furnishing of information where the consumer has notified the furnisher that the information is inaccurate and the information is in fact inaccurate).

[2] Experian – Oliver Wyman, *Comprehensive Consumer Credit Review, Experian-Oliver Wyman Market Intelligence Report*, at 7 (2011 Q4).

[3] See, e.g., Experian Connect[SM], available at http://www.experian.com/connect/landlord.html.

[4] Federal Trade Commission, *Credit-Based Insurance Scores: Impacts on Consumers of Automobile Insurance, A Report to Congress* (2007), available at http://www.ftc.gov/os/2007/07/P044804FACTA_Report_Credit-Based_Insurance_Scores.pdf.

[5] Marcie Geffner, *Banking and your credit score*, Bankrate.com (Mar. 17, 2011), available at http://www.bankrate.com/finance/savingsBanks may retrieve a credit report from a credit bureau as part of a review of a bank account application. A bank may also contact a specialty consumer reporting agency, like ChexSystems, a subsidiary of FIS, to see if the consumer has history of bank-initiated account closures or other negative activity in connection with previous checking accounts.

[6] The FCRA allows for the sharing of credit reports for employment purposes. See 15 U.S.C. § 1681b(a)(3)(B).

[7] Forty-seven percent of firms used credit checks for select job candidates, while thirteen percent used credit checks for all job candidates. The Society for Human Resource Management, *SHRM Research Spotlight: Credit Background Checks, Society Human Resource Management* (2010). Small, medium, and large employers were contacted as part of the survey. http://www.shrm.org/Research/SurveyFindings/Articles/Documents/CCFlier_FINAL.pdf. The CFPB, along with all other federal agencies, use credit reports in their employment screening process (specifically to check for any debts owed to the federal government).

[8] Federal Reserve Board, *Report to Congress on Credit Scoring and its Effects on the Availability and Affordability of Credit* (August 2007) (Board Credit Scoring Report), available at http://www.federalreserve.gov/boarddocs/rptcongress/creditscore/creditscore.pdf.

[9] 15 U.S.C. §1681e(b).

[10] 15 U.S.C. §1681c.

[11] Evan Hendricks, *Credit Scores and Credit Reports: How the System Really Works*, at 157 (2004).

[12] Id. at 158.

[13] Id.

[14] Based on CFPB calculations of industry publicly reported revenues.

[15] 15 U.S.C. § 1681a(d).

[16] 15 U.S.C. 1681a(g).

[17] Identifying information in credit files is derived from furnisher supplied data and from public records. Furnisher supplied identity information often comes directly from the consumer, and may vary depending on the identity information consumers provide on their

applications and how comprehensively the consumer and furnisher provide updates when such things as marital status, address, or phone number change. Identity information supplied in public records can also vary.

[18] John Ulzheimer, *Public Record Information and Credit Reports: What's There?*, Smartcredit.com, (March 3, 2011), available at http://www.smartcredit.com/blog/2011/03/03/public-record-information-and-credit-reports-whats-there/.

[19] 15 U.S.C. § 1681g(a)(3)(A).

[20] The FCRA's time limits on the reporting of derogatory information do not apply to certain large financial transactions, namely (1) a credit transaction involving, or which may reasonably be expected to involve, a principal amount of $150,000 or more; (2) the underwriting of life insurance involving, or which may reasonably be expected to involve, a face amount of $150,000 or more; or (3) the employment of any individual at an annual salary which equals or which may reasonably be expected to equal $75,000 or more. 15 U.S.C. § 1681c(b).

[21] 15 U.S.C. § 1681c(a)(4)-(5).

[22] 15 U.S.C. § 1681c(a)(2)-(3).

[23] 15 U.S.C. § 1681c(a)(1). As discussed supra, in note 20, reports may be exempted from these time restrictions in certain circumstances. In practice, the NCRAs do not utilize these exemptions, and cease reporting negative information after the standard time limits have elapsed.

[24] 15 U.S.C. § 1681c(a)(6).

[25] A credit score is a defined term in the FCRA which generally means "a numerical value or a categorization derived from a statistical tool or modeling system used by a person who makes or arranges a loan to predict the likelihood of certain credit behaviors, including default..." See 15 U.S.C. § 1681g(f)(2) for full definition.

[26] Board of Governors of the Federal Reserve System, Report to the Congress on Credit Scoring and Its Effects on the Availability and Affordability of Credit: Submitted to the Congress Pursuant to Section 215 of the Fair and Accurate Credit Transactions Act of 2003 (Aug. 2007), at O-4.

[27] One industry observer estimates that FICO had over 90 percent of the market share in 2010 of scores sold to firms for use in credit related decisions. Consumer Financial Protection Bureau, *The impact of differences between consumer- and creditor -purchased credit scores: Report to Congress*, at 6 (July 19, 2011).

[28] For more detailed information on the variety of credit score models sold to lenders and to consumers, see CFPB, "Analysis of Differences between Consumer- and Creditor-Purchased Credit Scores," (September 2012).

[29] New York Times, "Why you have 49 different FICO Scores," available at http://bucks.blogs

[30] See supra note 26 at O-5.

[31] Id.

[32] Deirdre Swesnik and Lisa Rice, National Fair Housing Alliance: Discriminatory Effects on Credit Scoring on Communities of Color, Prepared for the Symposium on Credit Scoring and Credit Reporting [forthcoming]

[33] Industry figures.

[34] Industry figures.

[35] Industry figures. It is likely that the NCRAs do not uniformly define an institution as a furnisher in the same way (e.g. some large, complex institutions may be treated as a single furnisher by one NCRA but as multiple furnishers by another); hence estimates cited in this report from industry sources about the number of furnishers and shares of tradelines by furnishers and industries are approximations.

[36] Industry information.

[37] The 2007 Economic Census provides the most comprehensive recent assessment of industry revenue concentration. The survey identifies 4,506 collection agencies. The largest of these firms (those with over $100 million in annual revenue) take in a minority proportion of

overall industry revenue (32%). See http://factfinder2.census.gov/faces/tableservices/jsf/pages/productview.xhtml?pid=ECN_2007_US_56SSSZ4&prodType=table# (scroll to NAICS code 56144).

[38] Historically, some furnishers have declined to provide certain fields. For example, omitting credit limits prompted the inclusion of I(b)(2) (iii) in App. E to the Furnisher Rule. 74 Fed. Reg. 31484 (July 1, 2009), available at http://www.gpo.gov/fdsys/pkg/FR-2009-07-01/pdf/E9-15323.pdf. The Furnisher Rule is now codified in 12 C.F.R. pt. 1022. 76 Fed. Reg. 79308 (Dec. 21, 2011). The practice of some furnishers of omitting account opening date and other fields also prompted the federal banking agencies, the National Credit Union Administration (NCUA), and the FTC to issue an advance notice of proposed rulemaking focused on whether furnishers should be required to provide this information, 74 Fed. Reg. 31529 (July 1, 2009), available at http://www.gpo.gov/fdsys/pkg/FR-2009-07-01/pdf/E9-15322.pdf.

[39] 74 Fed. Reg 31484 (July 1, 2009). This rule was required by section 623(e) of FCRA, as added by section 312 of the Fair and Accurate Credit Transaction Act of 2003.

[40] Industry information.

[41] Credit Advice from The "Ask Experian" Team, available at http://www.experian.com/ask-experian/20120118-what-derogatory-means.html

[42] Industry figures.

[43] Industry figures.

[44] Industry information.

[45] Industry figures.

[46] 74 Fed. Reg 31484 (July 1, 2009).

[47] 76 Fed. Reg. 79308 (December 21, 2011).

[48] 12 C.F.R. § 1022.42, (2012).

[49] 12 C.F.R. pt. 1022, Appendix E, III(h) (2012).

[50] 12 C.F.R. § 1022.42(a) (2012).

[51] 12 C.F.R. pt. 1022, Appendix E, III (2012).

[52] Industry figures.

[53] Ben Woolsey and Matt Schulz, *Credit card statistics, industry facts, debt statistics*, available at http://www.creditcards.com/credit-card- news/credit-card-industry-facts-personal-debt-statistics-1276.php (updated February 28, 2012).

[54] Industry figures. Since there are 1.3 billon trade lines updated every month and 200 million consumers in each of the NCRA databases, each consumer appears to have, on average, 6.5 active trade lines.

[55] Genealogy Data: Frequently Occurring Surnames from Census 2000. United States Census Bureau. Available at http://www.census.gov/genealogy/www/data/2000surnames/index.html.

[56] Industry information.

[57] Industry information.

[58] Federal Trade Commission, Report to Congress under Section 319 of the Fair and Accurate Credit Transaction Act of 2003, at 9 (December 2008).

[59] For a discussion of common credit reporting errors, see Richard J. Hilman, *Consumer Credit: Limited Information Exists on Extent of Credit Report Errors and Their Implications for Consumers*, Statement for the Record Before the Committee on Banking, Housing, and Urban Affairs, General Accounting Office at 11 (July 31, 2003).

[60] 15 U.S.C. § 1681i(a)(5)(C).

[61] In 2011, the FTC reported 279,156 complaints alleging identity theft, which was the largest single complaint category of consumers to the FTC. Federal Trade Commission, *Consumer Sentinel Network Data Book for January – December 2011*, at 6 (February 2012). See http://ftc.gov/sentinel/reports/sentinel-annual-reports/sentinel-cy2011.pdf.

[62] 15 U.S.C. §§ 1666-1666j.

[63] Industry figures.

[64] 15 U.S.C. § 1681i.
[65] 15 U.S.C. § 1681j(a) (requiring NCRAs and nationwide specialty consumer reporting agencies to provide free annual reports upon request if they have been providing consumer reports to third parties on a continuing basis with respect to consumers residing nationwide for the last 12 months).
[66] 15 U.S.C. §1681j(b).
[67] 15 U.S.C. § 1681j(c).
[68] Id.
[69] Id.
[70] 15. U.S.C. §1681j(d).
[71] Consumer Financial Protection Bureau, *The Impact of differences between consumer- and creditor-purchased credit scores: A Report to Congress,* at 9 (July 19, 2011).
[72] Id. at 10.
[73] Industry figures.
[74] Industry figures.
[75] Industry figures.
[76] Industry figures.
[77] Industry figures.
[78] Industry figures.
[79] 15 U.S.C. § 1681i(a)(1)(A).
[80] 15 U.S.C. § 1681i(a)(1)(B)-(C) and (a)(4).
[81] 15 U.S.C. 1681i(a)(2)(A).
[82] 15 U.S.C. 1681i(a)(2)(B).
[83] 15 U.S.C. 1681i(a)(5).
[84] 15 U.S.C. § 1681s-2(b); 12 C.F.R. pt. 1022, App. E.2b
[85] 12 C.F.R § 1022.43(a).
[86] 12 C.F.R. § 1022.43(e)(3).
[87] 12 C.F.R § 1022.43(e)(4).
[88] Industry figures.
[89] Id.
[90] Id.
[91] Finance companies, also known as personal finance or sales finance companies, are non-depository institutions that generally provide loans to higher risk borrowers, often to purchase retail items. An example might be a company that partners with a home retailer to provide a loan to a consumer to purchase bedroom furniture.
[92] Id.
[93] See The Federal Reserve, *An Overview of Consumer Data and Credit Reporting* (2003), at). 69. *See also* Jennifer Steinhauer, "Money & Medicine; Will Doctors Make Your Credit Sick?" *The New York Times*, February 4, 2011.
[94] *See* 12 C.F.R. § 1026.39 (2012).
[95] Industry figures.
[96] Id.
[97] Id.
[98] The Federal Trade Commission and the Board of Governors of the Federal Reserve System, *Report to Congress on the Fair Credit Reporting Act Dispute Process*, at 14 (August 2006).
[99] Industry figures.
[100] Industry figures.
[101] The Federal Trade Commission and the Board of Governors of the Federal Reserve System, *Report to Congress on the Fair Credit Reporting Act Dispute Process*, at 24 (August 2006).
[102] Stephen J. Hill, GAO Director of Financial Markets and Community Investment, Statement for the Record before the Committee on Housing, Banking, and Urban Affairs, U.S. Senate, "Consumer Credit: Limited Information Exists on the Extent of Credit Report Errors and their implications for Consumers, GAO-03-1036T (July 31, 2003).

[103] In-person briefing for CFPB staff on e-OSCAR with David Vaughn, General Manager, Central Source LLC and Stuart Pratt, President, CDIA (December 5, 2011).

[104] 15 U.S.C. § 1681i (a)(2)(B) (emphasis added).

[105] National Consumer Law Center, *Automated Injustice: How a mechanized dispute system frustrates consumers seeking to fix errors in their credit report,* at 23 (January 2009).

[106] Industry figures.

[107] Id.

[108] Michael A. Turner, PhD et al., *U.S. Consumer Credit Reports: Measuring Accuracy and Dispute Impacts*, the Policy & Economic Research Council (PERC), at 33 (May 2011).

[109] Id. at 37.

[110] Id. at 38.

[111] Id. at 39.

[112] Id. at 43.

[113] This calculation assumes that 200 million Americans have credit reports, and of these, 32 million have files that are too thin to score. Information Policy Institute, *Giving Underserved Consumers Better Access to the Credit System: The Promise of Non-Traditional Data*, at 7 (July 2005).

[114] Allison Cassady and Edmund Mierzwinski, *Mistakes do Happen: A Look at Errors in Consumer Credit Reports*, National Association of State PIRGs, at 4 (June 2004).

[115] Id. at 16.

In: The U.S. Credit Reporting System
Editor: Kendrick A. Minor ISBN: 978-1-62618-308-7

Chapter 2

PREPARED REMARKS ON CREDIT REPORTING BY RICHARD CORDRAY, DIRECTOR OF THE CONSUMER FINANCIAL PROTECTION BUREAU*

Thank you all for coming today. We are glad to be here in Detroit to hold this field hearing.

I myself am Midwestern born and bred, from neighboring Ohio, and received my undergraduate degree from Michigan State University, where I was a classmate of Magic Johnson and where I still have many lasting friends. So I am well aware that this state has suffered greatly in the last ten years with the one-two punch of lost manufacturing jobs and then the foreclosure crisis. People here, as in some other parts of the country, understand what it means to fight hard to find traction in a tough economy. After the financial crisis and extreme credit crunch of 2007-2008, tens of millions of Americans are now being pursued by debt collectors. Many people's credit ratings have taken a hit and now they are having a tough time regaining their financial footing. They are blocked from obtaining access to the credit that is often so essential to meaningful opportunity – to get an education, start a business, or buy a house.

We understand these realities at the Consumer Financial Protection Bureau because we hear about them from consumers every day. We also believe it is important to get out of Washington and listen directly to

* This is an edited, reformatted and augmented version of a Prepared Remarks Presented at the Credit Reporting Field Hearing in Detroit, Michigan on July 16, 2012. (Website information, http://www.consumerfinance.gov/ speeches/prepared-remarks-by-richard-cordray-on-credit-reporting/)

consumers by meeting them face to face. So we are glad to be with you today and to have you help us better understand how credit reporting companies (also called consumer reporting companies) affect people's daily lives for better and for worse.

These businesses track your credit history and payment records, and they analyze the information to determine what risks are posed by extending credit to you in the form of any kind of loan. Over the years, they have made it possible for a broad system of individual credit to grow and develop in this country, which has encouraged and promoted people's pursuit of the American dream of financial success. But, whether you realize it or not, their scorekeeping exerts a tremendous and growing influence over the ways and means of your financial lives. And so it is important for all of us to understand more about their work and the ways it can affect us.

Today, the Consumer Bureau is issuing a new regulation to expand our supervision program to oversee these credit reporting companies. The authority to supervise firms is the authority to conduct on-site examinations of whether and how they are complying with the law. It affords an opportunity to gain a more thorough understanding of their business models and their business practices, to work with them to correct any problems we find, and to find ways to resolve matters that may be causing harm to consumers.

Before we open this hearing, I want to take a few minutes to discuss the credit reporting market and our role in overseeing it. This is a field hearing. We are here to listen, to learn, and to gather on-the-ground information that will help inform our approach. We are thinking hard about issues in the credit reporting market, and we do not yet have all the answers worked out by any means. We need your help and your insight.

As Henry Ford once said, "If there is any one secret of success, it lies in the ability to get the other person's point of view and see things from that person's angle, as well as from your own." We believe in the wisdom of that statement. So, please, tell us what you think.

***

Let me start by talking about the credit reporting market.

Credit reporting plays a critical role in consumers' financial lives, a role that most people do not recognize because it is usually not very visible to them. Credit reports on a consumer's financial behavior can determine a consumer's eligibility for credit cards, car loans, and home mortgage loans – and they often affect how much a consumer is going to pay for that loan. If you have a credit record that appears to show a greater risk that you will fail to repay a loan, then you may be denied credit and you likely will be charged higher interest rates on any loan offered to you.

Our credit reporting system involves several key participants. First are the creditors and others that supply the information about your financial behavior, which can include your credit card issuers, your mortgage company, or companies that are collecting debts they claim you owe, among others. Second are those that collect and sell the information, which are the credit reporting companies. Third are those that use the information, which largely consist of financial institutions, but can also include insurance companies, auto dealers, retail stores, and even prospective employers. Fourth are consumers themselves, who are the object of all this scrutiny and who are immediately affected by it. All of these participants play important roles in ensuring that the credit reporting system operates effectively to help consumer credit markets work better for us all.

The credit reporting market is huge. Almost every adult in America has a credit file. Estimates are that each of the three biggest credit reporting companies maintains files on about 200 million Americans gleaned from over 10,000 providers of information. The amount of information collected and exchanged is astounding. Each year, approximately 3 billion credit reports are issued and more than 36 billion updates are made to consumer credit files.

A credit report contains information about the consumer's transactions – including loans that a consumer has paid on time, has paid late, has not paid, or has paid off, along with current amounts and sources of debt. The credit reporting companies also collect and report on information about consumers' finances available from public records, including civil judgments, liens, and bankruptcies from thousands of federal, state, and local courts and public offices.

The information contained in consumers' credit reports is used to derive their credit scores, such as various versions of the three-digit FICO score. Credit scores translate this great mass of information into a single number that indicates, in shorthand, a consumer's expected likelihood of repaying a loan. Generally, the lower the score, the lower a consumer's likelihood of repaying the loan compared to other consumers.

But credit reports are also used in a wide range of other types of decision-making – including determinations about eligibility for rental housing, what deposits are required for utility or telephone service, and premiums for auto and homeowners' insurance. Credit reports are even sometimes used to determine eligibility for a job. Banks, landlords, cell phone providers, and all kinds of other companies rely on the accuracy of this information to make good decisions and manage their risk of suffering losses.

Credit reporting is an important element in promoting access to credit that a consumer can afford to repay. Without credit reporting, consumers would not be able to get credit except from those who have already had direct experience with them, for example from local merchants who know whether or not they regularly pay their bills. This was the case fifty or a hundred years ago with "store credit," or when consumers really only had the option of going to their local bank. But now, consumers can instantly access credit because lenders everywhere can look to credit scores to provide a uniform benchmark for assessing risk. Conversely, credit reporting may also help reinforce consumer incentives to avoid falling behind on payments, or not paying back loans at all. After all, many consumers are aware that they should make efforts to build solid credit.

So this critical market is at the heart of our lending systems. It has enabled many of us to get credit and to afford a home or a college education.

But it is also clearly a market that can cause considerable problems for consumers. For example, sometimes credit reports contain errors that inaccurately reflect people's financial histories and can unfairly block them from getting approved for credit or can make it cost more than it should. Consumers also can encounter great difficulties at times in getting errors corrected. When the Consumer Bureau first opened its doors almost a year ago, we asked people to share their consumer experiences with us. We have heard reports since from many consumers that their credit reports are not accurate, and it is difficult to get them corrected. Because of the critical role that credit reports play in consumers' lives, it is our job to make sure we understand the full extent of these problems and address them effectively.

Given its enormity, given its influence, and given its wide impact on our overall economy, you can see that there is much at stake in ensuring that the credit reporting market is working properly for consumers.

***

Today the Consumer Bureau is announcing that we will be supervising the credit reporting companies that are the larger participants in this marketplace. These companies have never before been subject to a federal supervision program. Starting this September, we will be monitoring and examining them just as we monitor and examine the big banks. Our new supervision authority means that we will now have a clear window into the entire credit reporting system.

Up to this point, no single federal government agency could access all the information necessary to generate a complete picture of what was happening inside these companies. Now, the Consumer Bureau has the clear authority to oversee this industry, including the very largest credit reporting companies. Our oversight will also extend to specialty credit reporting companies, such as those that focus on payday loans or checking accounts, as well as resellers of credit reports and those that analyze credit report information. This new supervisory authority will complement our existing authority over the creditors that supply much of the information to the credit reporting companies.

Our country's credit system is a resource in which we all have much at stake – both directly and indirectly – and we need this system to operate effectively in order for the credit markets to work properly and fairly.

***

Because no federal agency has previously had the kind of broad access to information about the operations of the credit reporting companies that the Bureau will now have, there is much we do not know yet about the true risks that consumers face in this market. As we go forward, we will be gathering data to determine how the various parts of the Consumer Bureau can best act to protect consumers. We start with three areas of focus.

First, our oversight of the credit reporting companies will help us make sure that the information provided to them is itself reliable. Lenders and others who furnish information to the credit reporting companies are legally required to have policies in place about the accuracy and integrity of the information they report – which includes identifying consumers accurately, correctly recounting their actual payment history, and keeping their information and recordkeeping in order. Otherwise, their sloppy work becomes the true source of harm to the consumer's overall creditworthiness. We want to deepen our understanding of the recordkeeping and reporting practices by lenders and we want to see what the credit reporting companies can be doing to test and screen for the quality of information they receive.

Second, given the number of complaints we have already heard from consumers, and the findings reached in some (but not all) reports on the subject, we want and need to know more about the accuracy of how the credit reporting companies assemble and maintain the information contained in consumer credit reports. Accuracy is critical for consumers and for markets.

We recognize that achieving such accuracy takes a great deal of discipline and effort, particularly for a company that is handling and processing a huge volume of information. But because of the increasingly significant role these reports are taking on in our financial lives, the collateral consequences of mistakes can greatly harm consumers. The wrong information may cause them to be denied a loan, to be charged a much higher interest rate, or to be passed over for a job, causing them serious economic hardship. And inaccurate credit reports also deprive lenders of essential information they need to assess credit risk properly.

Third, we are keenly interested in understanding more about the problems and frustrations that consumers tell us they encounter in trying to resolve disputes about the information contained in their credit reports. Some errors may be unavoidable even in the best of systems. But when consumers find what they perceive to be erroneous information in their credit reports, they should not be burdened by unreasonably laborious processes to get errors removed from their files. There are certainly valid reasons why a credit reporting company must conduct a reasonable investigation when a consumer disputes information, and follow the procedures outlined in the law. But the harm done by errors is borne above all by consumers, and they deserve straightforward, effective, and timely mechanisms for addressing disputed items.

These initial areas of concern – accuracy of the information received by the credit reporting companies, their accuracy in assembling and maintaining that information, and the processes that govern error resolution – are just a start. They are the obvious and essential basics. But as we learn more about this market from consumers, from the supervised firms, and from others, we will adapt and adjust. The Fair Credit Reporting Act sets out an ambitious goal: Credit reporting companies "shall follow reasonable procedures to assure maximum possible accuracy of the information" contained in credit reports. In this context, we are here to correct what is not going well, and we are here to see that this market is made to work better for those who are affected the most. And we will exercise our supervisory authority to make sure that the consumer financial laws are being followed.

***

So the credit reporting industry is continuing to become more central to peoples' lives just at a time when they are experiencing widespread problems with credit availability. Many Americans have been greatly affected by the financial crisis, the housing crash, and the deep recession that followed. Today, because of accumulated debts, foreclosures, and bankruptcy filings, many people have more negative information on their credit reports than they did before the crisis. In fact, I am sure that some people in this audience, unfortunately, can attest to that.

As I said earlier, this country's credit reporting system is a resource in which we all have a stake. That system must merit our trust and confidence for the credit markets to be perceived as fair. We all share in this responsibility. But the credit reporting market is not one where consumers can shop around among different providers, for people have no choice about whether to have any of the credit reporting companies keep track of their credit history. That is why the Consumer Bureau's new authority is so important, and why it must be exercised carefully and effectively.

What consumers can do, however, is be smart about how they manage their own credit. They need to know how to build up their creditworthiness, so that they can take control over their credit history in a positive way. They also need to be aware that federal law gives them the right to a free credit report from each of the nationwide credit reporting companies – which can be obtained at www.annualcreditreport.com – once a year. It is critical for each of us to exercise that right. Keep in mind that nobody else has as much incentive to protect you as you have to protect yourself. Checking your credit report can reveal odd entries you do not recognize, which may be signs of identity theft. It also can uncover errors that will hurt your creditworthiness unless you dispute them and get them fixed. I urge every consumer to perform this self-check at least once every year. Starting today, we are including advice about how to do that in the "Ask CFPB" function on the Consumer Bureau's website at www.consumerfinance.gov. Our website also provides tips for consumers on how to manage their credit generally – how to get and keep a good credit score and how to navigate the consumer credit markets.

So as we wade in to these issues, we look forward to hearing more from you both today and in the future. Share your thoughts and experiences. We are intent upon hearing from consumers about their personal experiences to inform our work. To quote Henry Ford once again: "Coming together is a beginning; keeping together is progress; working together is success." Thank you.

In: The U.S. Credit Reporting System
Editor: Kendrick A. Minor

ISBN: 978-1-62618-308-7

Chapter 3

FAIR CREDIT REPORTING ACT: RIGHTS AND RESPONSIBILITIES*

Margaret Mikyung Lee

SUMMARY

The purpose of the Fair Credit Reporting Act (FCRA) is "to require that consumer reporting agencies adopt reasonable procedures for meeting the needs of commerce for consumer credit, personnel, insurance, and other information in a manner which is fair and equitable to the consumer, with regard to the confidentiality, accuracy, relevancy, and proper utilization of such information." The FCRA establishes consumers' rights in relation to their credit reports, as well as permissible uses of credit reports. It also imposes certain responsibilities on those who collect, furnish, and use the information contained in consumers' credit reports.

The FCRA has been amended several times over the last decade. The Fair and Accurate Credit Transactions Act of 2003 (FACT Act, P.L. 108-159) amended the FCRA to include a number of provisions aimed at preventing identity theft and assisting victims. The Credit Card Accountability Responsibility and Disclosure Act of 2009 (Credit CARD Act, P.L. 111-24) strengthened protections for young consumers and advertising disclosures regarding free credit reports from consumer reporting agencies. More recently,

* This is an edited, reformatted and augmented version of the Congressional Research Service Publication, CRS Report for Congress RL31666, dated February 2, 2012.

the Consumer Financial Protection Act of 2010, part of the Dodd-Frank Wall Street Reform and Consumer Protection Act (P.L. 111-203), established the Consumer Financial Protection Bureau and transferred administrative functions, including most rulemaking and reporting, as well as certain enforcement functions, from other federal agencies, such as the Federal Trade Commission and the Federal Reserve Board, to the Bureau.

This report discusses consumers' rights under the FCRA, as well as the type of information included in credit reports, permissible uses of credit reports, disclosure requirements, and requirements for users of consumer credit reports and furnishers of information. It also addresses FCRA provisions aimed at preventing identity theft and assisting victims of identity theft.

INTRODUCTION

The purpose of the Fair Credit Reporting Act (FCRA)[1] is "to require that consumer reporting agencies adopt reasonable procedures for meeting the needs of commerce for consumer credit, personnel, insurance, and other information in a manner which is fair and equitable to the consumer, with regard to the confidentiality, accuracy, relevancy, and proper utilization of such information."[2] The FCRA establishes consumers' rights in relation to their credit reports, as well as permissible uses of credit reports, disclosure requirements, and requirements for users of consumer credit reports and furnishers of information. The Fair and Accurate Credit Transactions Act of 2003 (FACT Act) amended the FCRA to include a number of provisions aimed at preventing identity theft and assisting victims.[3] The Credit Card Accountability Responsibility and Disclosure Act of 2009 (Credit CARD Act)[4] strengthened protections for young consumers and advertising disclosures regarding free credit reports from consumer reporting agencies. More recently, the Consumer Financial Protection Act of 2010,[5] part of the Dodd-Frank Wall Street Reform and Consumer Protection Act (Dodd-Frank Act),[6] established the Consumer Financial Protection Bureau (CFPB or the Bureau) and transferred administrative functions, including rulemaking and reporting, as well as certain enforcement functions, from other federal agencies such as the Federal Trade Commission and the Federal Reserve Board, to the Bureau.[7]

The FCRA applies to the files maintained by "consumer reporting agencies," a term broadly defined to include anyone in the business of furnishing reports on the creditworthiness of consumers to third parties.[8]

Consumer reporting agencies are also commonly known as credit bureaus or credit reporting agencies. A consumer reporting agency "is essentially a clearinghouse for information supplied by credit grantors and collection agencies, and culled by the bureau itself from public records."[9] In addition to several thousand small bureaus that often serve limited geographic areas, there are three major consumer reporting agencies that operate on a nationwide basis—Experian, Equifax, and Trans Union. Information on a particular consumer may be maintained by any one or all of the consumer reporting agencies serving a particular geographic area.

INFORMATION INCLUDED IN CONSUMER CREDIT REPORTS

Consumer credit reports generally include information about consumers' "credit worthiness [sic], credit standing, credit capacity, character, general reputation, personal characteristics, or mode of living."[10] The FCRA explicitly excludes certain types of financial reports from the definition of a consumer report. For example, "any report containing information solely as to transactions or experiences between the consumer and the person making the report" is excluded from the definition of consumer report, as are communications of that information among persons related by common ownership or affiliated by corporate control.[11] Authorizations or approvals of specific extensions of credit by the issuer of a credit card are also excluded from the definition of consumer report.[12]

With relatively few exceptions, there appears to be a consensus among the consumer reporting agencies as to the types of information that should be included in a report.[13] Information reported by a credit bureau commonly includes "identifying information, usually the individual's full name, Social Security number, address, telephone number, and spouse's name; financial status and employment information, including income, spouse's income, place, position, and tenure of employment, other sources of income, duration, and income in former employment; credit history, including types of credit previously obtained, names of previous credit grantors, extent of previous credit, and complete payment history; existing lines of credit, including payment habits and all outstanding obligations; public record information, including pertinent newspaper clippings, arrest and conviction records,[14] bankruptcies, tax liens, and lawsuits; and finally a listing of bureau subscribers that have previously asked for a credit report on the individual."[15]

The Fair Credit Reporting Act limits the amount of time that adverse or negative information can be included in a consumer's credit report. Generally, a credit reporting agency is prohibited from reporting adverse information that is more than seven years old, or in the case of bankruptcies, more than ten years old.[16] If a bankruptcy filed under title 11 of the United States Code is included on a consumer's report, the report shall also identify the chapter under which the case arose, if such information is provided by the source of the information.[17] If a bankruptcy case or filing under title 11 of the United States Code is withdrawn by the consumer before a final judgment, the report must include the fact that the case or filing was withdrawn.[18]

In addition to adverse credit information, consumer reporting agencies are also allowed to include information on a consumer's failure to pay overdue child support, if such information has been provided to the agency by a state or local child support enforcement agency or verified by any state or federal government agency. This information remains on the consumer report for up to seven years.[19]

Medical information may be included in consumer reports under certain circumstances and if consumer reporting agencies and creditors follow statutory and regulatory procedures and conditions to protect the confidentiality of such information.[20]

PERMISSIBLE USES OF CONSUMER CREDIT REPORTS

The Fair Credit Reporting Act outlines the purposes for which a consumer credit report may be furnished to a requester.[21] In general, a consumer reporting agency may furnish a copy of a consumer's report to a person the agency has reason to believe intends to use the information for the purpose of extending credit to the consumer or for reviewing or collecting of the consumer's credit account.[22] Consumer credit reports may also be issued where there is another "legitimate business need" for the information contained in the report in connection with a business transaction initiated by the consumer, or for purposes of reviewing an existing account to determine whether the consumer continues to meet the terms of the account.[23] Reports may be furnished to executive branch departments and agencies in connection with the issuance of government-sponsored travel charge cards that are billed to employees.[24] An insurer may receive a report in connection with the underwriting of an insurance policy involving the consumer for which the consumer has applied.[25] Various other uses are permitted, including, among others, a response to a court order, a decision regarding a consumer's employment, and determination by a government agency of a consumer's ability to make child support payments.[26]

Reports may be issued in connection with transactions not initiated by the consumer only if authorized by the consumer, or if the transaction is a firm offer for credit or insurance and the consumer has not elected to have his name removed from lists provided by the agency for this purpose.[27] A consumer may elect to have his name removed from such lists by notifying the reporting agency that he does not consent to the release of reports for this purpose.[28] If the consumer has not authorized the release of such reports and has not elected to have his name removed from the lists, the agency may release only certain information about the consumer. Information released in connection with transactions not initiated by the consumer is limited to the name and address of the consumer, an identifier that is not unique to the consumer and that is used solely for the purpose of verifying the consumer's identity, and other information pertaining to the consumer that does not identify his/her relationship or experience with respect to a particular creditor or other entity.[29] The Credit CARD Act of 2009 added protections from prescreened offers for persons under 21 years of age. Credit reports for such consumers cannot be issued in connection with such offers unless the consumer has consented.[30]

In addition to reports issued for the commercial purposes discussed above, a consumer reporting agency may also issue a report to a person it has reason to believe "intends to use the information in connection with a determination of the consumer's eligibility for a license or other benefit granted by a governmental entity required by law to consider an applicant's financial responsibility or status."[31]

The FCRA also authorizes consumer credit reports to be released for certain legal purposes. Specifically, the act authorizes consumer credit reports to be released "in response to the order of a court having jurisdiction to issue such an order," or in response to "a subpoena issued in connection with proceedings before a Federal grand jury."[32] Reports may also be issued to state or local child support enforcement agencies if needed to establish the consumer's capacity to pay child support or to determine the amount of such payments.[33]

If certain requirements are met, reports may also be issued for employment purposes.[34] In order to obtain a report for employment purposes, the requester must certify that the report will not be used in violation of any state or federal law.[35] The consumer must be told by the prospective employer that a report may be obtained and must consent to the procurement of a report by the employer.[36] If the employer intends to take adverse action based in whole or in part on the report, the consumer must be provided with a copy of the report and a description of the rights afforded to consumers under the FCRA.[37]

A consumer report may also be issued to the Federal Deposit Insurance Corporation or the National Credit Union Administration as part of its powers, as conservator, receiver, or liquidating agent for an insured depository institution or insured credit union or in connection with the resolution or liquidation of a failed or failing insured depository institution or insured credit union.[38]

CONSUMER RIGHTS

The Fair Credit Reporting Act outlines consumers' rights in relation to their credit reports. Under the FCRA, consumers have the right to access all information in their credit reports, including the sources of the information, and the right to disclosure of their credit scores.[39] A consumer may request one free credit report, not including a free credit score, each year from each of the nationwide consumer reporting agencies.[40] Pursuant to an amendment by the Credit CARD Act of 2009,[41] advertisements for a free credit report in any medium, including television, radio, and the internet, must include a disclosure to the effect that free annual reports are available under federal law at "AnnualCreditReport.com" or other sources authorized by federal law and that the privately advertised service is not the free report required by law. Free reports may also be obtained under certain circumstances, such as notice of an adverse action based on information in a credit report or a consumer's request for a credit report in conjunction with a fraud alert.[42] Absent one of these circumstances, a consumer may be charged up to $11.00 for additional copies of his or her credit report.[43] Except in certain circumstances, a consumer reporting agency may charge a fair and reasonable fee, as determined by the Bureau ($11.00 maximum), for providing a consumer's current credit score or the one most recently calculated for an extension of credit.[44] This paid disclosure must include a notice that the credit score purchased by the consumer may differ from a score purchased and used by a lender or other user of credit reports and scores.[45] As required by the Dodd-Frank Act, the Bureau issued a report in 2011 on the nature, range, and size of variations between credit scores sold to creditors and those sold to consumers by consumer reporting agencies and whether such variations disadvantage consumers.[46]

In addition to the disclosure of information contained in the consumer's credit report, a consumer is also entitled to receive information identifying each person who obtained a consumer credit report for employment purposes during the previous two years, or for any other purpose during the previous year.[47] Additional information that must be disclosed to the consumer upon request includes "the dates, original payees, and amounts of any checks upon which is based any adverse characterization of the consumer, included in the file at the time of the disclosure;" and "a record of all inquiries received by the agency during the one-year period preceding the request that identified the consumer in connection with a credit or insurance transaction that was not initiated by the consumer."[48]

Consumers have the right to dispute the completeness or accuracy of information contained in their files.[49] Once a consumer notifies the consumer reporting agency of the dispute, the agency must reinvestigate and record the current status of the disputed information, or delete it from the consumer's file within 30 days.[50] The consumer reporting agency must also notify the furnisher of the disputed information of the consumer's dispute and provide the furnisher with all relevant information the agency has received from the consumer regarding the dispute.[51]

In conducting the reinvestigation, the consumer reporting agency must review and consider all relevant information submitted by the consumer.[52] The agency may terminate the reinvestigation if it reasonably determines that the dispute is frivolous or irrelevant, or if the consumer fails to provide sufficient information to investigate the disputed information.[53] Should the agency determine that the dispute is frivolous or irrelevant, it must notify the consumer of the determination not later than five business days after making such determination.[54] If the reinvestigation leads to a determination that the disputed information is in fact inaccurate, incomplete, or unverifiable, the consumer reporting agency must delete that item of information from the consumer's credit file.[55]

The consumer reporting agency must provide written notice of the results of the reinvestigation to the consumer within five days of completing the reinvestigation.[56] The notice must include a statement that the reinvestigation is completed; a copy of the consumer report reflecting the information in the consumer's file revised during the reinvestigation; a notice that, if requested by the consumer, a description of the procedure used to determine the accuracy and completeness of the information can be provided; a notice that the consumer has the right to add a statement to his/her file disputing the accuracy or completeness of the information contained therein; and a notice that the consumer has the right to request that the consumer reporting agency send notices regarding deleted information to specified parties.[57]

RESPONSIBILITIES OF CONSUMER REPORTING AGENCIES

Certain provisions of the Fair Credit Reporting Act are aimed at ensuring that the information in consumers' credit files is accurate and complete. As discussed above, under the FCRA, consumer reporting agencies must conduct a reasonable reinvestigation if a consumer disputes the accuracy of any information in his/her file.[58] The agencies also must notify requesters of consumer reports of any substantial discrepancies between the address the agency has on file for a consumer and the consumer's address included in the request.[59]

In addition to their responsibilities related to the accuracy of information in consumers' files, credit reporting agencies must also ensure that consumer credit reports are released only for the purposes discussed above.[60] In order to ensure that the reports are used for permissible purposes, the credit reporting agencies must require that the prospective users of the information identify themselves, certify the purposes for which the information is sought, and certify that the information will be used for no other purpose.[61]

Consumer reporting agencies also have a duty to notify furnishers of information in the files and users of consumer reports of their responsibilities under the FCRA.[62]

In addition to the general responsibilities discussed above, a consumer reporting agency has responsibilities with regard to investigative consumer reports and reports provided for employment purposes. Prior to collecting information for or preparing an investigative consumer report, the agency must disclose to the consumer the nature and scope of the requested investigation and the fact that such a report may be made.[63] A consumer reporting agency may not prepare or furnish an investigative consumer report unless it has received certification from the requesting party that the required disclosures have been made to the consumer.[64] With regard to reports prepared for employment purposes, a consumer reporting agency must take precautions to insure the accuracy of public record information that may be included in the report.[65] The consumer must be notified that such information is being reported and be given the name and address of the person to whom the information is being reported; or the agency must "maintain strict procedures designed to insure that whenever public information which is likely to have an adverse effect on the consumer's ability to obtain employment is reported it is complete and up to date."[66]

RESPONSIBILITIES OF FURNISHERS OF INFORMATION

Many types of businesses and organizations contribute information to consumers' credit files. The major credit reporting agencies classify contributors of information into the following categories: "automobile dealers; banks, clothing, department, and variety stores; finance agencies; grocery and home furnishing dealers; insurers; jewelry and camera stores; contractors; lumber, building materials, and hardware suppliers; medical-care providers; national credit card companies and airlines; oil companies (credit card divisions); personal services other than medical; mail-order houses; real estate agents; hotel keepers; sporting goods and farm and garden supply dealers; utilities; fuel distributors; government agencies (e.g. the Federal Housing Administration and the Veterans Administration); wholesalers; advertisers; and collection agencies."[67]

Generally, any person who has information related to a consumer's financial activities can report information about that person's transactions and experiences with the consumer to a consumer reporting agency. However, a person or business with information about a consumer is not required to report that information to a consumer reporting agency. If negative information is reported, the furnisher must notify the consumer in writing.[68]

Persons who furnish information to consumer reporting agencies have a duty to provide accurate information. Under the FCRA, a furnisher may not provide any information relating to a consumer to a consumer reporting agency if the person knows or has reasonable cause to believe that the information is inaccurate.[69] Furnishers of information are also prohibited from furnishing information if they have been notified by the consumer that the information they are reporting is inaccurate.[70] Furnishers are also prohibited from furnishing information identified by the consumer as resulting from identity theft, unless the furnisher subsequently knows or is informed by the consumer that the information is correct.[71] The FCRA requires furnishers of information to have in place reasonable procedures to prevent information resulting from identity theft from being refurnished after notification from a consumer reporting agency that such information is being blocked because it resulted from identity theft.[72]

In addition to the reinvestigation requirements imposed on consumer reporting agencies, furnishers of information are also required to investigate disputed information. After a furnisher of information receives notice from a consumer reporting agency regarding disputed information in a consumer report, the person furnishing the information must investigate and report the results to the consumer reporting agency.[73] If the furnisher finds that the information is incomplete or inaccurate, the furnisher must report those results to all other consumer reporting agencies to which the incomplete or inaccurate information was furnished.[74] Furnishers of information must also notify consumer reporting agencies when an account is closed by the consumer, and when delinquent accounts are being placed for collection, charged to profit or loss, or subjected to any other similar action.[75]

The FCRA also allows consumers to dispute the accuracy of information directly with the furnisher. Furnishers must investigate the disputed information and report the results to the consumer within a specified period of time.[76] If the information is found to be inaccurate, the furnisher must notify each consumer reporting agency to which the information was originally furnished and provide the correct information.[77]

Requirements for Users of Consumer Reports

As noted above, consumer credit reports can be used only for the purposes specified in the Fair Credit Reporting Act. Despite these limitations, users of consumer credit reports vary widely. The most common users of consumer reports are credit grantors, such as credit card companies. Other common users include insurers, employers, collection agencies, and government agencies.[78] The FCRA imposes specific requirements on persons who use the information contained in consumer reports.

Users of consumer reports must follow the requirements set forth in the Fair Credit Reporting Act if they take any adverse action with respect to any consumer that is based in whole or in part on any information contained in the consumer's report.[79] If such action is taken, the user must provide the consumer with oral, written, or electronic notice of the adverse action.[80] The notice must include the name, address, and telephone number of the consumer reporting agency that furnished the report to the user; and a statement that the consumer reporting agency did not take the adverse action and is unable to provide the consumer with specific reasons why the adverse action was taken.[81] The consumer must also be notified of his or her right to obtain a free copy of the consumer report from the consumer reporting agency that furnished the report and of the consumer's right to dispute the accuracy or completeness of that report.[82] The consumer must also be given written or electronic disclosure of a credit score used in any adverse action based in whole or in part on any information in the consumer report, including the range of credit scores, the factors adversely affecting the score, the date the score was created, and the provider of the credit score.[83]

A notice must also be provided by users who grant, extend, or otherwise provide credit on material terms that are materially less favorable than the most favorable terms available to a substantial proportion of consumers from or through that user.[84] The notice must inform the consumer that the terms offered to the consumer were set based on information from a consumer report; identify the consumer reporting agency that furnished the report; inform the consumer that he or she may obtain a free copy of the consumer report from that agency; provide the contact information specified by the agency for obtaining such reports; and provide the credit score used in deciding the credit terms, the range of credit scores, the factors adversely affecting the score, the date the score was created, and the provider of the credit score.[85]

The FCRA also imposes duties on users of consumer reports when reports are used in connection with a credit or insurance transaction not initiated by the consumer. Written solicitations made to consumers regarding credit or insurance transactions not initiated by the consumer must include a "clear and conspicuous statement" that information from the consumer's credit report was used in connection with the transaction; the consumer received the offer for credit or insurance because he or she satisfied specified criteria; and the credit or insurance may not be extended if, after the consumer responds to the offer, the consumer does not meet additional criteria used to determine creditworthiness or insurability.[86] The statement must also inform the consumer of his/her right to prohibit information contained in his/her file from being used in connection with any transaction he/she did not initiate and how he/she may exercise this right.[87]

IDENTITY THEFT PROVISIONS

The FCRA includes a number of provisions aimed at preventing identity theft and assisting victims of identity theft.[88] These provisions mirror laws passed by state legislatures and create a national standard for addressing consumer concerns with regard to identity theft and other types of fraud.[89] They impose responsibilities on consumer reporting agencies, furnishers of information, and users of consumer credit reports, and provide consumers with rights for protecting the information in their files and insuring that the information contained in them is accurate.

Credit card issuers are required to follow certain procedures when they receive a request for an additional or replacement card within a short period of time following notification of a change of address for the same account.[90] In a further effort to prevent identity theft, credit card account numbers must be truncated on electronically printed receipts,[91] and, upon request, social security numbers must be truncated on credit reports provided to a consumer.[92] Because hundreds of apparently frivolous lawsuits were being brought for willful noncompliance where the expiration date of a credit card was on a receipt although the number was truncated and there was no allegation of injury to consumers, a 2008 amendment to the FCRA clarified that the mere printing of the expiration date did not constitute willful noncompliance if the receipt otherwise complied with the FCRA.[93]

Consumers who have been victims of identity theft, or expect that they may become victims, can have fraud alerts placed in their files.[94] A consumer may request a fraud alert from one consumer reporting agency and that agency is required to notify the other nationwide consumer reporting agencies of the alert.[95] In general, fraud alerts are to be maintained in the file for 90 days, but a consumer may request an extended alert which is maintained for up to seven years. The fraud alert becomes a part of the consumer's credit file and is thus passed along to all users of the report. The alert must also be included with any credit score generated using the consumer's file.[96]

In addition to the fraud alert, victims of identity theft may have information resulting from the crime blocked from their credit reports.[97] After receiving proof of the consumer's identity, a copy of an identity theft report, the identification of the alleged fraudulent information, and a statement by the consumer that this particular information does not relate to any transaction he/she conducted, a consumer reporting agency must block this particular information from being reported and must notify the furnisher of the information in question that it may be the result of identity theft. Requests to block information must also be referred to other consumer reporting agencies.[98]

Victims of identity theft may request information about the alleged crime. A business entity is required, upon request and subject to verification of the victim's identity, to provide copies of application and business transaction records evidencing any transaction alleged to be a result of identity theft to the victim without charge or to any law enforcement agency investigating the theft and authorized by the victim to receive the records in question.[99]

Pursuant to FACT Act amendments in 2003,[100] the federal agencies regulating the financial services industry promulgated guidelines and regulations, known as the Red Flags Rule, requiring financial institutions and creditors to establish reasonable policies and procedures to prevent identity theft.[101] The Red Flags Rule had an effective date of January 1, 2008, and a mandatory compliance date of November 1, 2008, but the mandatory compliance date was delayed several times due in part to controversy over the scope of entities covered by the rule as creditors.[102] The final mandatory compliance date was December 31, 2010, permitting time for Congress to enact the Red Flag Program Clarification Act of 2010,[103] clarifying that creditors covered by the rule do not include businesses that advance funds for expenses incidental to the services they offer, such as lawyers, doctors, dentists, etc. Creditors subject to the rule are entities that "regularly and in the ordinary course of business" obtain credit reports in connection with credit transactions, furnish information to consumer reporting agencies in connection with credit transactions, and extend credit based on an obligation to repay.

End Notes

[1] P.L. 91-508, Title VI, §601, 84 Stat. 1128 (1970), codified as amended at 15 U.S.C. §§1681–1681x.

[2] 15 U.S.C. §1681(b).

[3] P.L. 108-159, 117 Stat. 1952. These provisions are discussed in detail *infra* at Identity Theft Provisions. More information on these provisions and other issues related to identity theft can be found in CRS Report R40599, *Identity Theft: Trends and Issues*, by Kristin M. Finklea; CRS Report RL31919, *Federal Laws Related to Identity Theft*, by Gina Stevens. For information on data security generally and related legislative proposals, see CRS Report RL34120,*Federal Information Security and Data Breach Notification Laws*, by Gina Stevens, and CRS Report RL33273, *Data Security: Federal Legislative Approaches*, by Gina Stevens.

[4] P.L. 111-24, 123 Stat. 1734 (2009).

[5] P.L. 111-203, Title X, §§1001–1100H, 124 Stat. 1376–2113 (2010).

[6] P.L. 111-203, 124 Stat. 1376 (2010).

[7] *Id.*, §§1024-1027, 1029, and 1061 provide for the certain functions of the CFPB and the transfer of functions from the other federal financial services agencies and the Federal Trade Commission to the CFPB. The changes to administrative enforcement authority for the FCRA made by §1088 of the Dodd-Frank Act are codified at 15 U.S.C.§1681s. The Dodd-Frank Act did not transfer to the Bureau the rulemaking authority for the Red Flag guidelines and regulations pursuant to 15 U.S.C. §1681m(e) and for the disposal of records pursuant to 15 U.S.C. §1681w. Also, the Federal Trade Commission retained rulemaking authority over auto dealers pursuant to §1029 of the Dodd-Frank Act. Pursuant to §1024(c)(3) of the Dodd-Frank Act, the CFPB and the FTC recently concluded a Memorandum of Understanding to establish a framework for coordinating enforcement and regulatory efforts, available at http://www.ftc.gov/os/2012/01/120123ftc-cfpb-mou.pdf, press release available at http://www.ftc.gov/opa/2012/01/ftccfpb.shtm. Regulation V, the Fair Credit Reporting regulations, are now at 12 C.F.R. part 1022, part of the CFPB regulations, promulgated at 76 Fed. Reg. 79308 (2011).
For more information on the transfer of functions to the CFPB, see CFPB, *Streamlining Inherited Regulations*, 76 Fed. Reg. 75825 (2011); CFPB, *Identification of Enforceable Rules and Orders*, 76 Fed. Reg. 43569 (2011); CFPB, *Agencies Issue Statement to Clarify Supervisory and Enforcement Responsibilities For Federal Consumer Financial Laws,* at http://www.consumerfinance.gov/pressrelease/agencies-issue-statement-to-clarify-supervisory-and-enforcement-responsibilities-for-federal-consumer-financial-laws; and CRS Report R41338, *The Dodd-Frank Wall Street Reform and Consumer Protection Act: Title X, The Consumer Financial Protection Bureau*, by David H. Carpenter. The Federal Trade Commission issued a report on its experiences administering and enforcing the FCRA, *Forty Years of Experience with the Fair Credit Reporting Act: An FTC Staff Report and Summary of Interpretations* (2011), while simultaneously rescinding its official staff interpretations in the Code of Federal Regulations, in anticipation of the transfer of certain regulatory functions to the CFPB, report and rescission available at http://www.ftc.gov/opa/2011/07/fcra.shtm.

[8] 15 U.S.C. §1681a(f). The FCRA defines a consumer reporting agency as "any person which, for monetary fees, dues, or on a cooperative nonprofit basis, regularly engages in whole or in part in the practice of assembling or evaluating consumer credit information or other information on consumers for the purpose of furnishing consumer reports to third parties, and which uses any means or facility of interstate commerce for the purpose of preparing or furnishing consumer reports."

[9] Frederick H. Miller, et al., *Consumer Law: Cases, Problems, and Materials*, p. 296.

[10] 15 U.S.C. §1681a(d)(1).

[11] 15 U.S.C. §1681a(d)(2)(A). "The first type of excluded information [among persons related by common ownership] is information based on first hand experience of one of the affiliates. The second type [among persons affiliated by corporate control] is any other information shared by affiliates, provided that the sharing is disclosed to the consumer and the consumer is given the opportunity to direct that the information not be shared among related entities." Debtor-Creditor Law §16.02[3] (Matthew Bender & Co. 2011).

[12] 15 U.S.C. §1681a(d)(2)(B).

[13] Miller, *supra* note 9.

[14] Experian does not maintain information concerning criminal records; see http://www.experian.com/credit-education/credit-report-faqs.html.

[15] Miller, *supra* note 9.

[16] 15 U.S.C. §1681c(a). The seven- and ten-year reporting limitations do not apply to transactions involving, or which may be expected to involve, an amount greater than $150,000; the underwriting of life insurance involving, or which may involve, an amount of $150,000 or more; or to the employment of any individual at an annual salary which equals, or may be expected to equal, more than $75,000. 15 U.S.C. 1681c(b). Information regarding certain

types of student loans may be reported until the loan is paid in full. 20 U.S.C. §1087cc(c)(3).

[17] 15 U.S.C. §1681c(d).

[18] *Id.*

[19] 15 U.S.C. §1681s-1.

[20] FACT Act of 2003, P.L. 108-159, §§411 and 412, 117 Stat. 1999-2003, amending 15 U.S.C. §§1681a(d)(3) and (i), 1681b(g), 1681c(a)(6), and 1681s-2(a)(9).

[21] 15 U.S.C. §1681b.

[22] 15 U.S.C. §1681b(a)(3)(A).

[23] 15 U.S.C. §1681b(a)(3)(F).

[24] 15 U.S.C. §1681b(a)(3)(G).

[25] 15 U.S.C. §1681b(a)(3)(C). For more information on the use of consumer credit information by the insurance industry, see CRS Report RS21341, *Credit Scores: Credit-Based Insurance Scores*, by Baird Webel.

[26] 15 U.S.C. §1681b(a).

[27] 15 U.S.C. 1681b(c)(1). This provision allows "prescreening" by a consumer reporting agency. "Prescreening" is the process "whereby a consumer reporting agency compiles or edits a list of consumers who meet specific criteria and provides this list to the client or third party on behalf of the client for use in soliciting these consumers for the client's products or services." Prescreening is permissible under the Fair Credit Reporting Act if the client agrees in advance that each consumer on the list will receive an offer of credit. See CCH Consumer Credit Guide, ¶ 25,050.

[28] 15 U.S.C. §1681b(e). Pursuant to the 2003 amendment to the FCRA, persons who use consumer reports for prescreening purposes must provide the consumer with a statement including the address and telephone number where the consumer may request to be excluded from prescreened lists. The consumer's election to be excluded from such lists is effective for five years. FACT Act of 2003, P.L. 108-159, §213, 117 Stat. 1978, codified as amended at 15 U.S.C. §1681m(d)(2).

[29] 15 U.S.C. §1681b(c)(2).

[30] 15 U.S.C. §1681b(c)(1)(B)(iv); subparagraph (iv) was added by the Credit CARD Act of 2009, P.L. 111-24, §302, 123 Stat. 1748.

[31] 15 U.S.C. §1681b(a)(3)(D).

[32] 15 U.S.C. §1681b(a)(1).

[33] 15 U.S.C. §1681b(a)(4). In order for reports to be released for this purpose, the paternity of the consumer must have been established or acknowledged by the consumer; the consumer must be given notice of the request; and the report must be kept confidential and used only for this purpose. Id.

[34] 15 U.S.C. §1681b(a)(3)(B). Under the FCRA, "employment purposes" mean "a report used for the purpose of evaluating a consumer for employment, promotion, reassignment or retention as an employee." 15 U.S.C. §1681a(h).

[35] 15 U.S.C. §1681b(b)(1).

[36] 15 U.S.C. §1681b(b)(2).

[37] 15 U.S.C. §1681b(b)(3).

[38] 15 U.S.C. §1681b(a)(6).

[39] 15 U.S.C. §1681g(a). Credit scores must be made available to consumers pursuant to an amendment in the FACT Act of 2003, P.L. 108-159, §212(a), (b), 117 Stat. 1973, codified as amended at 15 U.S.C. §1681g(a), (f). Prior to this amendment, consumer reporting agencies were under no obligation to release credit scores. For a discussion of how credit scores are used, see CRS Report RS21298, *Credit Scores: Development, Use, and Policy Issues*, by Pauline Smale.

[40] 15 U.S.C. §1681j(a), as amended by the FACT Act of 2003, P.L. 108-159, §211(a), 117 Stat. 1968. For more information on free credit reports, see CRS Report RL32008, *A Consumer's Access to a Free Credit Report: A Legal and Economic Analysis*, by Loretta Nott and Angie

A. Welborn. The free credit report is not required to include the consumer's credit score. The credit score must be disclosed upon request, but a reasonable fee may be imposed for the disclosure. P.L. 108-159, §212(b), 117 Stat. 1973-1975, codified as amended at 15 U.S.C. §1681g(f)(8).

[41] Section 205 of the Credit CARD Act of 2009, *supra* note 4, codified as amended at 15 U.S.C. §1681j(g); this requirement responded to consumer confusion about whether certain free credit reports, offered by consumer reporting agencies in conjunction with the sale of other credit information or monitoring services, were the statutorily required free annual reports. See also the related rule at 12 C.F.R. §1022.138.

[42] See 15 U.S.C. §1681j(b), (c), and (d).

[43] 15 U.S.C. §1681j(f) and Federal Trade Commission, *Charges for Certain Disclosures*, 75 Fed. Reg. 80817 (2010)(notice of the annual adjustment, based on the Consumer Price Index, of the maximum reasonable fee that can be charged for disclosures under 15 U.S.C. §1681g, other than the free annual credit report and notices and disclosures required by the FCRA). Section 1088 of the Dodd-Frank Act, *supra* note 6, transferred the responsibility for the annual fee adjustment to the CFPB (see 15 U.S.C. §1681j(f)(2)), but it has not yet adjusted the fee for 2012.

[44] *Id.* and 15 U.S.C. §1681g(f)(8). Certain mortgage lenders must disclose to a consumer the credit score used for the purpose of the loan; 15 U.S.C. §1681g(g). Also, as discussed *infra* notes 83 and 85, when users of credit reports take an adverse action or offer credit on terms less favorable than usual, they must disclose the credit score on which such actions were based.

[45] 15 U.S.C. §1681g(f)(1).

[46] Section 1078 of the Dodd-Frank Act, *supra* note 6, required the study and report by the Bureau, *Report to Congress: The impact of differences between consumer- and creditor-purchased credit scores*, available at http://www.consumerfinance.gov/report/the-impact-of-differences-between-consumer-and-creditor-purchased-credit-scores.

[47] 15 U.S.C. §1681g(a)(3).

[48] 15 U.S.C. §1681g(a)(4), (5).

[49] 15 U.S.C. §1681i.

[50] 15 U.S.C. §1681i(a)(1)(A).

[51] 15 U.S.C. §1681i(a)(2)(A).

[52] 15 U.S.C. §1681i(a)(4).

[53] 15 U.S.C. §1681i(a)(3)(A).

[54] 15 U.S.C. §1681i(a)(3)(B).

[55] 15 U.S.C. §1681i(a)(5).

[56] 15 U.S.C. §1681i(a)(6)(A).

[57] 15 U.S.C. §1681i(a)(6)(B).

[58] 15 U.S.C. §1681i(a)(1)(A).

[59] 15 U.S.C. §1681c(h).

[60] 15 U.S.C. §1681e(a)

[61] *Id.*

[62] 15 U.S.C. §1681e(d). For discussions of the responsibilities of furnishers of information and users of credit reports, see relevant sections following in this report.

[63] 15 U.S.C. §1681d(a), (b).

[64] 15 U.S.C. §1681d(d).

[65] 15 U.S.C. §1681k.

[66] 15 U.S.C. §1681k(a)(1), (2).

[67] Miller, *supra* note 9, p. 298.

[68] 15 U.S.C. §1681s–2(a)(7).

[69] 15 U.S.C. §1681s–2(a)(1).

[70] *Id.*

[71] 15 U.S.C. §1681s–2(a)(6).

[72] *Id.*
[73] 15 U.S.C. §1681s-2(b)(1).
[74] *Id.*
[75] 15 U.S.C. §1681s-2(a)(4), (5).
[76] 15 U.S.C. §1681s-2(a)(8(E).
[77] *Id.*
[78] For descriptions of how each uses the information contained in consumer reports, see Miller, *supra* note 9, pp. 300– 301.
[79] In general, an adverse action is any negative action, such as a denial or termination, taken with respect to the consumer's application or continued coverage for credit, insurance, or employment. The FCRA provides a detailed definition of adverse action at 15 U.S.C. §1681a(k).
[80] 15 U.S.C. §1681m(a)(1).
[81] 15 U.S.C. §1681m(a)(3). Particular requirements relate to adverse actions based on information received from third parties other than consumer reporting agencies. These requirements generally impose a duty on the user to disclose the reasons for the adverse action and the nature of the information received from the third party. See 15 U.S.C. 1681m(b).
[82] 15 U.S.C. §1681m(a)(4).
[83] 15 U.S.C. §1681m(a)(2); the requirement for credit score disclosure was added by §1100F of the Dodd-Frank Act, *supra* notes 5 and 6.
[84] 15 U.S.C. §1681m(h)(1).
[85] 15 U.S.C. §1681m(h)(5). The subparagraph requiring credit score disclosure (15 U.S.C. §1681m(h)(5)(E)) was added by §1100F of the Dodd-Frank Act, *supra* notes 5 and 6.
[86] 15 U.S.C. §1681m(d)(1).
[87] Id. See also 15 U.S.C. §1681b(e).
[88] For more information on identity theft issues and the Red Flags Rule, discussed *infra*, see CRS Report R40599, *Identity Theft: Trends and Issues*, by Kristin M. Finklea.
[89] Generally, many of these federal provisions preempt similar state laws. For more information on the preemptive effects of the Fair Credit Reporting Act, see CRS Report RS21449, *Fair Credit Reporting Act: Preemption of State Law*, by Margaret Mikyung Lee.
[90] 15 U.S.C. §1681m(e)(1)(C). These are part of the Red Flag guidelines and rules designed to prevent identity theft.
[91] 15 U.S.C. §1681c(g).
[92] 15 U.S.C. §1681g(a)(1)(A).
[93] Credit and Debit Card Receipt Clarification Act, P.L. 110-241, §3(a), 122 Stat. 1565 (2008) (codified at 15 U.S.C. 1681n(d)). The U.S. Supreme Court recently granted certiorari to United States v. Bornes, No. 11-192 (January 13, 2012), http://www.supremecourt.gov/orders/courtorders%5C011312zr.pdf, to decide whether the Little Tucker Act, 28 U.S.C. 1346(a)(2), waives the sovereign immunity of the United States with respect to damages actions for violations of the FCRA. The federal government allegedly violated the FCRA prohibition against printing the expiration date of a consumer's credit card on a receipt provided at the point of sale or transaction. The plaintiff/respondent had received electronic internet and email receipts displaying the expiration date of the personal credit card he used to pay government filing fees for a client's lawsuit.
[94] 15 U.S.C. §1681c-1.
[95] 15 U.S.C. §§1681c-1(a)(1)(B) and 1681s(f)(1).
[96] 15 U.S.C. §1681c-1(a)(1)(A).
[97] 15 U.S.C. §1681c-2.
[98] 15 U.S.C. §1681s(f)(1).
[99] 15 U.S.C. §1681g(e).
[100] Section 114 of the FACT Act, *supra* note 3, made amendments codified at 15 U.S.C. §1681m(e).

[101] 72 Fed. Reg. 63718 (2007). The Dodd-Frank Act did not transfer authority to prescribe regulations with regard to the Red Flags requirements to the CFPB; such authority is retained by the federal banking agencies as well as the National Credit Union Administration, the Federal Trade Commission, the Commodity Futures Trading Commission, and the Securities and Exchange Commission.

[102] See 156 Cong. Rec. H8059-60 (daily ed. December 7, 2010); 156 Cong. Rec. S8288-89 (daily ed. November 30, 2010); Federal Trade Commission, *FTC Extends Enforcement Deadline for Identity Theft Red Flags Rule* (2010), at http://www.ftc.gov/opa/2010/05/redflags.shtm; Federal Trade Commission, *FTC Extends Enforcement Deadline for Identity Theft Red Flags Rule* (2009), at http://www.ftc.gov/opa/2009/10/redflags.shtm.

[103] P.L. 111-319, 124 Stat. 3457 (2010), codified at 15 U.S.C. §1681m(e)(4).

In: The U.S. Credit Reporting System
Editor: Kendrick A. Minor
ISBN: 978-1-62618-308-7

Chapter 4

REPORT TO CONGRESS ON THE FAIR CREDIT REPORTING ACT DISPUTE PROCESS*

Federal Trade Commission and the Board of Governors of the Federal Reserve System

EXECUTIVE SUMMARY

The Federal Trade Commission ("FTC") and the Board of Governors of the Federal Reserve System ("Board") submit this report pursuant to section 313(b) of the Fair and Accurate Credit Transactions Act of 2003 ("the FACT Act"). The report discusses the steps that consumer reporting agencies ("CRAs") and furnishers of information to CRAs ("furnishers") take after receiving a consumer dispute about the accuracy or completeness of information in the consumer's file. The report first provides background information and describes the Fair Credit Reporting Act's ("FCRA's") dispute provisions. The core portion of the report, titled "The Dispute Process," addresses (1) how the consumer submits a dispute to the CRA, (2) how the CRA forwards the dispute to the furnisher, (3) how the furnisher investigates the dispute and replies to the CRA, and (4) how the CRA reviews the furnisher's response and conveys the results of the reinvestigation to the

* This is an edited, reformatted and augmented version of the Federal Trade Commission, Board of Governors of the Federal Reserve System, dated August 2006.

consumer. The report also discusses the dispute process when consumers submit disputes directly to furnishers. The Board issued a request for public comment, and the report summarizes commenters' overall views on the dispute process.

The report finds that, although the materials that the FTC and the Board reviewed indicated that most disputes seem to be processed within the statutory time frame, there is disagreement as to the adequacy of the CRAs' and furnishers' investigations. The FACT Act imposes a number of new requirements to enhance the consumer dispute process. These provisions are still being implemented.

As a result, this report is based solely on compliance with the pre-FACT Act FCRA dispute process and recommends no additional administrative or legislative action at this time.

The FTC and the Board believe that the FACT Act requirements should be given time to take effect before legislators and regulators consider making additional changes to the dispute process. The FTC and the Board will continue to monitor the performance of the dispute process, explore possible enhancements, and make recommendations for action, if appropriate.

I. INTRODUCTION

The Federal Trade Commission ("FTC") and the Board of Governors of the Federal Reserve System ("Board") submit this report pursuant to section 313(b) of the Fair and Accurate Credit Transactions Act of 2003 ("the FACT Act").[1] Section 313(b) of the FACT Act, enacted on December 4, 2003, mandates that the FTC and Board jointly study

> [t]he extent to which, and the manner in which, consumer reporting agencies and furnishers of consumer information to consumer reporting agencies are complying with the procedures, time lines, and requirements under the Fair Credit Reporting Act for the prompt investigation of the disputed accuracy of any consumer information, the completeness of the information provided to consumer reporting agencies, and the prompt correction or deletion, in accordance with such Act, of any inaccurate or incomplete information or information that cannot be verified.

Section 313(b) also requires that the FTC and the Board submit a joint report on the results of the study. In preparing the report, the two agencies must consider information relating to complaints filed with the FTC and referred to the nationwide consumer reporting agencies under section 611(e) of the Fair Credit Reporting Act ("FCRA").[2]

Lastly, section 313(b) requires that the report include any recommendations that the Board and the FTC jointly determine to be appropriate for legislative or administrative action.

In preparing this report, the FTC and the Board drew upon information provided by various sources. The Board issued a request for public comment on the topics required by section 313(b).[3] The two agencies reviewed over 120 comment letters received from consumers,[4] consumer advocates,[5] creditors and their trade associations,[6] consumer reporting agencies ("CRAs") and their trade associations,[7] and mortgage industry trade associations.[8] The comment letters are available on the FTC's website, at www.ftc.gov/os/statutes.

The FTC and the Board also met with consumer advocates and groups representing CRAs and furnishers. In addition, the FTC and the Board reviewed consumer complaint information maintained within their own databases and those of several other federal financial regulators.[9] The Board reviewed information gained through examinations for FCRA compliance by several federal financial regulators.

Finally, the FTC and the Board reviewed the existing literature, including studies, reports, and industry manuals, as well as research conducted by the Board's staff economists. This report summarizes the information provided by these sources. Part II discusses the role of CRAs and furnishers in the dispute process, describes consumer reports, and explains the relevant provisions of the FCRA. Because the process by which information is furnished to CRA databases is important to understanding the dispute process, Part III of this report discusses reporting responsibilities and the systems through which furnishers report information to CRAs.

Part IV discusses the various steps that consumers, CRAs, and furnishers take during the dispute process, the systems used to exchange information between CRAs and furnishers when consumers dispute information contained in their consumer files, as well as commenters' overall views on how well the dispute process is working.

Part V of the report discusses FCRA enforcement by the FTC, the Board, and other federal agencies; consumer complaints reviewed by the Board and several other federal agencies; and the complaint-referral program that the FTC has entered into with CRAs in compliance with FCRA section 611(e). Finally, Part VI contains the report's conclusions.

II. BACKGROUND

A. The Actors

The FCRA dispute process involves CRAs and those who furnish information to the CRAs. The largest CRAs are three nationwide "repositories" of consumer credit information: Equifax Information Services, LLC ("Equifax"), Experian Information Solutions, Inc. ("Experian"), and TransUnion LLC ("TransUnion").[10] Each repository has records on as many as 1.5 billion credit accounts held by approximately 210 million individuals.[11] According to the Consumer Data Industry Association (CDIA), the repositories receive approximately 4 billion updates of information each month from more than 30,000 furnishers,[12] and normally update their credit records within one to seven days of receiving new information.[13] The repositories issue more than 1 billion consumer reports each year, the vast majority of which go to creditors, employers, and insurers.[14] In 2003, the most recent year for which figures are available, the repositories issued 57.4 million consumer file disclosures, i.e., reports sent to consumers at their request.[15]

The term "consumer reporting agency" in the FCRA covers many entities other than the three repositories.[16] For example, the repositories report that approximately twenty companies, traditionally referred to as "service bureaus" or "affiliates," have contractual relationships with one of the repositories under which the affiliate owns consumer data in certain areas of the country but stores the data on the repository's computer.[17] Other entities that fall within the definition of "consumer reporting agency" include those that collect and report specialized information, such as check writing histories, rental records, employment histories, and medical information.[18]

Another category of CRAs, "resellers," purchase consumer information from one or more of the repositories, provide further input to the consumer report, including merging files from multiple repositories or adding information from other data sources, and then resell the report.[19] While this report briefly describes the changes in reseller dispute duties under the FACT Act and includes comments from their trade representatives, the focus of the report with respect to CRAs will be on the repositories, which own and maintain the vast majority of the data held by CRAs.

Unlike "consumer reporting agency," the term "furnisher" is not defined in the FCRA. As the term is generally understood, however, furnishers are entities that provide information about their customers to CRAs, including information about customers' payments on their accounts. Examples of furnishers include banks, thrifts, credit unions, savings and loan institutions, mortgage lenders, credit card issuers, collection agencies, retail installment lenders, and auto finance lenders.[20] The FCRA does not require furnishers to report to CRAs, but, as discussed below, if they do report, they must comply with certain provisions of the statute. According to CDIA, the majority of furnishers report full account payment information, both "positive" information that the account is current and "negative" information, such as delinquencies and accounts placed for collection.[21] Some types of accounts are typically reported only when the payment history turns negative, such as when the debt is transferred to a debt collector. The most common examples of these accounts are those related to medical debts, telecommunications, and power companies.[22]

B. Consumer Reports

Full consumer reports issued by the repositories, commonly referred to as "credit reports," generally contain five types of information:[23]

- *Identification Information*: Information such as the name of the individual, current and previous residential addresses, and Social Security number.
- *Trade Line Information*: Detailed information reported by creditors and other furnishers on each current and past loan, lease, or other debt (such as utility and medical debts).
- *Public Record Information*: Information derived from financial-related public records, such as records of bankruptcies, foreclosures, tax liens, garnishments, and other civil judgments.
- *Collection Account Information*: Information reported by collection agencies regarding credit accounts and other debts.
- *Inquiry Information*: Identities of individuals or companies that have requested information from an individual's credit file; the date of inquiry; and an indication of whether the inquiry was by the consumer, for the review of an existing account, or to help the inquirer decide on a potential future account or relationship.

Although Equifax, Experian, and TransUnion are for-profit businesses that compete with one another on, among other things, the completeness of the information in their databases, many items in a consumer's files are common to all three repositories. This is due in large part to the standard formats that furnishers use to report information to the repositories.[24] Nonetheless, some differences remain across repositories. Some furnishers, including some smaller banks and many debt collection agencies, do not report to all three repositories.[25] Differences also can arise from the repositories' treatment of public record information. Because some public record information is accessible only by visiting courthouses and other government buildings in person, the repositories sometimes hire contractors to gather the information.[26] When repositories use different contractors, the contractors sometimes report the same public record information differently, causing additional variations among repository databases.[27] Yet another reason that repositories' databases differ is that the repositories often receive and process information from furnishers at different times during the same reporting cycle.[28]

C. FCRA Dispute Duties

The FCRA imposes dispute duties on both CRAs and furnishers. If a consumer disputes the completeness or accuracy of an item contained in his or her file directly with the CRA,

- the CRA must complete a reinvestigation within thirty days after receiving the notice of dispute from the consumer;[29]
- in conducting the reinvestigation, the CRA must review and consider all relevant information submitted by the consumer; and[30]
- within five business days of receiving the dispute, the CRA must notify the furnisher of the dispute, and include all relevant information that the CRA received from the consumer.[31]

After receiving a dispute from a CRA, a furnisher must take the following steps:[32]

- conduct an investigation with respect to the disputed information;
- review all relevant information provided by the CRA;
- report the results of the investigation to the CRA;
- if the investigation finds that the information is incomplete or inaccurate, report those results to all nationwide CRAs to which the furnisher reported the information; and

- complete the investigation before the end of the thirty-day period that the CRA has to complete its reinvestigation.

If the CRA finds during the reinvestigation that a disputed item is inaccurate, incomplete, or cannot be verified, the CRA must delete or modify the item.[33] No later than five business days after the completion of a reinvestigation, a CRA must provide written notice to the consumer of the results of the reinvestigation.[34] The notice must include

- a statement that the reinvestigation is completed;
- a consumer report based on the consumer's file (if the file has been revised as a result of the reinvestigation);
- a notice that the CRA will provide a description of the procedure used to determine the accuracy and completeness of the disputed item to the consumer at the consumer's request;
- a notice that the consumer has the right to add a statement to his or her file disputing the accuracy or completeness of the information; and
- a notice that the consumer has the right to request that the CRA furnish notification that the item had been deleted, or the consumer's statement of dispute, to certain persons designated by the consumer who had previously received a consumer report that contained the deleted or disputed information.

The FACT Act amended the FCRA in a number of ways that affect the consumer dispute resolution process.[35] One of the changes requires the FTC, the Board, and other federal agencies to promulgate guidelines and regulations requiring creditors to establish reasonable procedures regarding the accuracy of the data they report to CRAs.[36] A second change also requires joint regulations identifying the circumstances under which furnishers, for the first time, must investigate certain disputes received directly from consumers.[37] A third FACT Act change requires that, in disputes received from a CRA, if information disputed by a consumer is found to be inaccurate or incomplete or cannot be verified after the furnisher completes the investigation, the furnisher must promptly delete, modify, or permanently block the reporting of that information, as appropriate based on the results of the investigation.[38] The FACT Act amendments also require financial institutions that furnish information to nationwide CRAs to notify consumers in writing if they furnish, or may furnish, negative information about the consumers to a CRA.[39] Because these and other provisions of the FACT Act have not become effective or have only recently become effective, this report focuses on the dispute process as it existed under the FCRA prior to the FACT Act amendments.

III. The Reporting Process

This section provides an overview of the process through which furnishers report information to the CRAs. According to CDIA, more than 30,000 furnishers provide approximately 4 billion updates of information to the repositories each month.[40] In general, financial services providers such as banks, credit unions, and consumer finance companies provide the majority of positive and negative account information in CRA files.[41]

A. Reporting Requirements

The FCRA does not require furnishers to report to CRAs. Some entities that choose to furnish, however, are required by the FCRA to report certain information. For example, a furnisher must notify a CRA if the consumer voluntarily closes a credit account that the furnisher has been reporting to that CRA.[42] The FCRA also requires a furnisher that provides information to a CRA regarding a delinquent account being placed for collection, charged off, or subjected to similar action, to notify the CRA of the month and year that the delinquency began.[43]

Some entities are required to furnish certain information due to contractual or other requirements. For example, the Mortgage Bankers Association (MBA) stated that "[m]ost mortgage companies … are required by investors and government entities, such as Fannie Mae, Freddie Mac, and [the U.S. Department of Housing and Urban Development], to report 'full file' credit information," including both positive and negative information and the exact status of each mortgage serviced as of the last business day of each month, to each of the repositories.[44]

Nevertheless, because the FCRA generally does not require reporting, some furnishers choose not to report at all, to report only negative information, or to omit a key element of data such as a credit limit.[45] Others report data on some of their credit products and not others.[46] Commenters proffered a variety of reasons why some furnishers choose not to report or to report only certain kinds of information. CDIA reported that "[s]ome lenders omit the reporting of very elite customers out of concern that other lenders will attempt to compete for this market of consumers."[47] Other lenders choose not to report their subprime portfolios for the same reason.[48] Some regulated entities, such as telephone companies, are limited by regulations as to the types of information they may report to CRAs.[49] Some of these companies, for example, are permitted to report only information about accounts that are in past due or charged-off status.[50] Some entities choose not to report to all the repositories in light of the potential liability imposed on furnishers by the FCRA dispute provisions as well as the costs involved in furnishing.[51] These costs may include those associated with reporting, handling investigation requests, establishing policies and procedures to ensure compliance with the FCRA, and performing audits of reporting systems and information reported.[52]

B. Reporting Formats

Most furnishers use one of two standard formats to report credit information to the repositories. In the mid-1970's, the credit reporting industry developed the Metro format, which was designed to ensure greater precision in the data reported to the CRAs.[53]

In 1997, CDIA introduced the Metro 2 format.[54] Metro and Metro 2 each provide a standard format, including standard codes, that can be used for virtually any consumer credit transaction. According to CDIA, Metro 2 is "an updated and more robust version of Metro, and provides for complete and accurate reporting."[55]

For example, unlike the Metro format, Metro 2 allows a furnisher to report complete identification information for each consumer, including co-debtors and co-signers, which makes it more likely that CRAs will match the reported item to the correct consumer's file.[56] The repositories currently receive over 99% of all data from furnishers in either the Metro or Metro 2 format.[57] Approximately 31% of these furnishers—representing approximately 50% of all data furnished to the repositories—now report through Metro 2.[58] The repositories hope to convert the rest of the furnishers to Metro 2.[59]

Repositories also obtain information from courts, city halls, tax offices, and motor vehicles departments.[60] For those public record sources that are not yet available electronically, the repositories often hire contractors to manually collect the information.

This information is then added to the repositories' databases for inclusion in future consumer reports.[61]

IV. The Dispute Process

In the consumer dispute process, a consumer first reviews his or her credit report and identifies information in the report that he or she believes is incomplete or inaccurate. The consumer then communicates a dispute to the CRA, which conveys the dispute to the furnisher of the information. The furnisher investigates the dispute and reports back to the CRA the results of its investigation. Finally, the CRA communicates the outcome of the reinvestigation to the consumer. In some cases, consumers communicate a dispute directly to the furnisher.[62] This section will discuss each step of the dispute process, as well as the commenters' overall views on how well the current process is working.

A. Consumer Reviews Consumer Report and Conveys Dispute to CRA

In a 2004 Government Accountability Office (GAO) survey of 1578 consumers, 58% of consumers had seen their credit report at some point, and 45% of this subgroup had viewed their report within the previous year.63 Of the 58% who had viewed their report at some point, 53% said they had ordered their report themselves, and 47% said someone else (e.g., a mortgage company, financial institution, or car dealership) had ordered their report and given it to them.[64] CDIA reported that the repositories issued 57.4 million file disclosures (i.e., reports sent to consumers at their request) in 2003.[65] If a consumer requests a credit report from one of the nationwide CRAs, the CRA must provide the consumer with a toll-free telephone number at which personnel are accessible to consumers during normal business hours.[66]

The 58% of consumers in the GAO study who had seen their credit report at some time gave the following as the reasons their credit report had been ordered:[67]

48%	Making a large purchase or refinancing
30%	Checking for completeness and accuracy
8%	Due to an adverse action, such as denial of credit, based on a credit report
4%	Suspected fraud and/or identity theft
1%	Looking for a job
9%	Other reasons

A consumer who believes that an item reported in a credit report is inaccurate or incomplete may contact the CRA by mail, online, by telephone, or in person to dispute the item.[68] According to CDIA, of the 57.4 million file disclosures issued to consumers by the repositories in 2003, 21.8% (12.5 million) led to a reinvestigation by one of the repositories.[69] Approximately 18% of the consumers interviewed in the GAO survey said that they disputed information in their credit file at some point.[70] The consumers surveyed by GAO reported the following reasons for their disputes:[71]

17%	Someone else's information
14%	Incorrect payment history
14%	Incorrect late payments
13%	Incorrect bill information
13%	Incorrect credit card information
10%	Incorrect personal information
7%	Incorrect balance information
4%	Incorrect bankruptcy information
3%	Incorrect information from a former spouse
2%	Identity theft
4%	Another reason

To understand how often credit accounts are disputed, the Federal Reserve Board reviewed data provided by one of the three repositories as of June 30, 2003.[72] The data are broken out by percentage of accounts in dispute. The Board found that 0.18% of credit accounts had a pending dispute.[73] Most of the disputes related to open accounts (85.4% of the pending disputes related to open accounts and 14.6% related to closed accounts).[74] Of those credit accounts in dispute, 89.9% were credit card accounts.[75]

B. CRA Processes Dispute

As discussed above, when a consumer submits a dispute to a CRA, the CRA generally must reinvestigate within thirty days.[76] As part of the reinvestigation, the CRA must review and consider all relevant information submitted by the consumer.[77] Although the FCRA before the FACT Act did not specifically state that a CRA's reinvestigation had to be "reasonable," courts generally imposed a reasonableness standard. Under the FACT Act, the FCRA now expressly requires that a CRA's reinvestigation be reasonable.[78]

Whether a particular CRA's actions constitute a "reasonable" reinvestigation varies depending on the circumstances surrounding the dispute.[79]

The joint comment letter submitted by the National Consumer Law Center, Consumer Federation of America, Consumers Union, Electronic Privacy Clearinghouse, and U.S. Public Interest Research Group ("the consumer groups") asserted that CRAs fail to conduct meaningful reinvestigations and merely "parrot" information received from furnishers as "verified," without independently investigating the accuracy and completeness of such information.[80] CDIA, on the other hand, maintained that the repositories meet their obligations to perform reinvestigations. According to CDIA, in some cases the CRA makes the correction without even submitting the dispute to the furnisher. CDIA asserted that the repositories "examine the information provided by a consumer, and where that information demonstrates that the account should be changed or deleted, the account is changed or deleted."[81] Similarly, TransUnion claimed that, "if the documentation [provided by a consumer] can be reasonably verified as being authentic, the account is automatically updated based on the documentation, in lieu of sending" a dispute to the furnisher.[82]

C. CRA Forwards Dispute to Furnisher

Assuming the CRA does not resolve the dispute itself, the CRA must provide notice of the dispute to the entity that furnished the disputed information, along with "all relevant information regarding the dispute that the CRA has received from the consumer," within five business days after receiving the consumer's dispute.[83]

1. How CRA Conveys Dispute to Furnisher

When a consumer contacts a CRA to dispute information on the consumer's credit report, the consumer generally is asked to provide the name of the furnisher that reported the disputed item, the account number relating to the disputed information, the reason for the dispute, and certain identifying information (e.g., date of birth, Social Security number, and current address).[84] A CRA employee typically fills out a consumer dispute verification ("CDV") form based on the information the consumer provides. The CRA either sends the CDV to the furnisher via mail or fax, or electronically in the form of an Automated Consumer Dispute Verification ("ACDV"). (An example of an ACDV form is attached as appendix B.) After investigating the disputed information, the furnisher fills in relevant portions of the CDV or ACDV and returns it to the CRA.

CRAs and furnishers also communicate through Universal Data Forms (“UDFs”). Like CDVs and ACDVs, UDFs are used by furnishers to notify CRAs that information the furnisher has reported should be deleted or modified in some way. Unlike CDVs and ACDVs, however, UDFs are initiated by furnishers, rather than by CRAs. For example, if a consumer contacts a furnisher directly to dispute the accuracy of an item that the furnisher has reported to a CRA, and the furnisher determines that the information is inaccurate, the furnisher generally would use a UDF to notify the CRA of the inaccuracy.[85] UDFs sent electronically are referred to as Automated Universal Data forms (“AUDs”).

The credit reporting industry’s current electronic dispute processing system is known as e-OSCAR[86] (“Online Solution for Complete and Accurate Reporting”). The system is web-based and permits furnishers to receive and send ACDVs, and send AUDs, over the Internet.[87] On the ACDVs they send through e-OSCAR, CRAs provide the furnisher with identifying information about the consumer in the CRA’s file; one or two codes summarizing the consumer’s dispute; and, if the CRA deems it necessary, a free-form narrative field that supplements the dispute codes.[88] CRAs select the dispute codes from among twenty-six offered by the e-OSCAR system, such as “Not his/hers” and “Claims account closed.” CDIA provided the full list of codes to the FTC and the Board but declined to release the list for use in this report, citing concerns that the codes are confidential and that credit repair organizations would misuse their knowledge of the dispute codes to have accurate information removed from consumers’ files.[89]

According to CDIA, as of December 2004, e-OSCAR had nearly 15,400 registered users[90] and more than 83% of all disputes were being processed on the e-OSCAR system.[91] The remaining disputes currently are processed through paper CDVs. When a consumer contacts a repository to dispute an item reported by a furnisher that does not participate in e-OSCAR, the repository submits a paper CDV by mail or fax to the furnisher that reported the disputed data. The furnisher investigates the disputed data and returns the paper CDV to the repository, which then uses the information to update the consumer’s file as necessary.[92] Some CRAs convey disputes to furnishers through telephone calls. While repositories generally do not use this method,[93] resellers often do, conducting three-way calls with the consumer and the furnisher that reported the disputed item.[94] According to the National Credit Reporting Association (NCRA), a trade association that represents many resellers, resellers generally are willing to provide disputes to furnishers by whatever means the furnisher demands.[95]

Each of the three repositories, however, has announced plans to stop accepting paper-based disputes and require all furnishers to participate in e-OSCAR.[96] MBA commented that it is unclear whether all mortgage servicers or other creditors have access to e-OSCAR.[97] Several furnishers have responded to the repositories' plans to stop accepting paper-based disputes by stating that they will refuse to pay the fee to use e-OSCAR.[98] As a result, these furnishers argue, any disputed information that they report will be deleted because the furnisher has no other way to respond to the dispute.[99] To avoid this, MBA recommended in its comment letter that there be a free alternative to e-OSCAR for CRAs to accept corrections from furnishers.[100]

2. "All Relevant Information"

As noted above, when CRAs send disputes to furnishers, the FCRA requires them to include "all relevant information regarding the dispute that the agency has received from the consumer."[101] Comments reflected differing views on whether the current system sufficiently provides "all relevant information" for all disputes. The consumer groups commented that consumers often supply CRAs with information and documentation sufficient to support their disputes (including account applications, billing statements, and letters), but CRAs neither review the documentation nor forward it to furnishers.[102] The consumer groups asserted that the twenty-six dispute codes CRAs use in ACDVs and CDVs to describe consumer disputes convey only "generic descriptions" of the disputes.[103]

A number of furnishers commented that the dispute codes are "vague and broad," and that the CRAs do not always provide sufficient information.[104] The Coalition to Implement the FACT Act reported that a significant volume of current disputes—according to some Coalition members, 30%–40% of all disputes—are assigned generic, or "catch-all," dispute codes, such as "other" or "consumer complains data inaccurate; no specific dispute." According to the Coalition, the use of these catch-all codes makes investigations time-consuming and costly.[105] At the same time, most furnishers reported that the information provided to them through e-OSCAR usually is sufficient to investigate the dispute.[106] According to CDIA, the free-form field is used in 30% of all disputes processed through e-OSCAR.[107] MBA also noted that, while the information its members receive from CRAs is often cursory, it generally is not problematic, adding that the bank can contact the borrower directly for information.[108]

According to CDIA, the e-OSCAR system as it currently exists already conveys all relevant information.[109] The two repositories that submitted comments, TransUnion and Equifax, agreed.[110] CDIA reported that 22% of consumer disputes submitted to the repositories are submitted by telephone,[111] and that many other disputes are submitted on the standardized form that CRAs provide when they give consumers copies of their consumer reports. Thus, CDIA commented, most disputes are not accompanied by additional relevant information.[112] TransUnion also reported that most consumer disputes it receives do not reference or contain any specific information or documentation.[113] CDIA added that, "due to credit repair activity or even individual choices, not all information or documentation that a consumer submits is truthful or authentic, nor are all requests for reinvestigations valid."[114]

TransUnion stated that it typically does not supply copies of consumer-supplied documentation to furnishers but added that, "if the documentation can be reasonably verified as being authentic, the account is automatically updated based on the documentation, in lieu of sending an ACDV or CDV."[115] Equifax noted that it currently provides two methods of supplementing the e-OSCAR dispute codes and free-form field: (1) a copy of the documentation can be faxed to the furnisher as appropriate and (2) furnishers can contact CRAs with questions they have about a particular dispute.[116]

In April 2006, CDIA stated that its members "have continued to research both the technological and legal questions that might arise from providing consumer-submitted information directly to data furnishers." It concluded that "the viability of the concept of making consumer-submitted information available through the e-OSCAR system to data furnishers is now questionable."[117]

D. Furnisher Investigates and Sends Response to CRA

1. Furnisher's Investigation

A furnisher that receives notice of a dispute from a CRA is required to

(A) conduct an investigation with respect to the disputed information;

(B) review all relevant information provided by the consumer reporting agency...;

(C) report the results of the investigation to the consumer reporting agency; and

(D) if the investigation finds that the information is incomplete or inaccurate, report those results to all other [nationwide] consumer reporting agencies to which the person furnished the information.[118]

Whether a furnisher's actions constitute a sufficient investigation depends on a number of factors, including the information the furnisher received about the dispute and the steps the furnisher takes to investigate the dispute.[119]

According to the consumer groups, "regardless of where the dispute is made (directly with the furnisher or through a CRA), furnishers are simply *not* conducting meaningful reinvestigations; they do *not* train their employees on effective reinvestigation procedures; and they repeatedly default simply to verifying the existence of an account."[120] The consumer groups assert that furnishers rarely research the underlying dispute, review documents, or analyze the furnishers' own data for inconsistencies and errors.[121]

Other commenters provided varying information on the level of investigation that furnishers conduct in response to disputes. Several furnishers commented that they compared the information provided on the dispute notice with the information contained in the furnishers' records.[122] Wells Fargo and Company (Wells Fargo) indicated that such information could include the

- consumer's name, address, and Social Security number;
- consumer's account number;
- account payment history;
- account servicing notes and collection notes;
- loan documents; and
- deferral, modification, and extension history.[123]

Similarly, Zions Bancorporation (Zions) indicated that its consumer loan servicing department researches the account history to match the consumer's identifying information and to determine the timing of the payment compared to the payment due dates.[124] If the department's staff members determine that they reported incomplete or inaccurate information, they send a correction to CRAs through the e-OSCAR system.[125]

Some commenters stated that furnishers generally correct their internal records to ensure that the incorrect information is not re-reported to CRAs.[126] In some cases, the furnisher will also send a letter to the consumer indicating that the information was incomplete or inaccurate and that a correction will be made.[127] NAMB asserts, however, that some furnishers do not correct their internal records, and, as a result, the incorrect information is reinserted into the consumer's file at the CRA the next time the furnisher sends an electronic update to the CRA.[128] As amended by the FACT Act, however, the FCRA now requires furnishers to delete, modify, or permanently block the reporting of disputed information that is found to be inaccurate or incomplete or cannot be verified.[129] This change is likely to reduce the instances of incorrect information being reinserted.

2. Furnisher Communicates Results to CRA

If a furnisher determines that the information in dispute is neither incomplete nor inaccurate, the furnisher generally selects "Verified as Reported" on the ACDV or CDV and returns it to the CRA.[130] If, instead, the furnisher determines that the information the consumer disputed is incomplete or inaccurate, the furnisher generally makes the correction on the ACDV or CDV and returns it to the CRA.[131] If the furnisher is using e-OSCAR, the system forwards the information automatically to any other nationwide CRA to which the furnisher reported the disputed item.[132] According to CDIA, e-OSCAR also edits for illogical furnisher responses and provides furnishers with an error message if the data they enter in responding to a dispute are inconsistent with the dispute code.[133] MBA commented that disputes returned to CRAs through e-OSCAR are more quickly reflected in consumers' credit reports than are disputes conveyed to CRAs through paper.[134]

In contrast to the experience of the repositories, the National Credit Reporting Association commented that where the dispute has been reported to a reseller and then forwarded to the furnisher, furnisher practice varies. Some furnishers provide the correct information to the reseller and then forward the correction to the proper repository. Other furnishers do not respond at all, causing the reseller to delete the disputed information, whether it is accurate or not.[135] The FACT Act amended the FCRA to no longer require resellers to forward disputes to the furnisher that reported the disputed item. Instead, resellers generally are permitted to forward the consumer dispute to the CRAs from which they obtained the disputed item ("source CRA").[136] The source CRA then must reinvestigate the dispute as if it had come directly from the consumer. This new process is likely to alleviate the problems that the NCRA described.

If a consumer continues to dispute information after the formal dispute process has been concluded, some furnishers offer the consumer the option of submitting additional evidentiary information that the furnishers then review.[137] Under the FCRA, the consumer has a right to include a statement of dispute in the consumer report if the reinvestigation does not resolve the dispute.[138] Several furnishers commented that they advise consumers of this option, although some commenters questioned its value.[139] TransUnion reported that approximately 4% of all consumer file disclosures result in a statement of dispute being added to the file after the repository completed its reinvestigation.[140] Of the 18% of consumers in the GAO survey who disputed information in their file and either (1) the information was not deleted from their files or (2) they did not know whether the information was deleted, 30% submitted such a dispute statement to the CRA.[141]

3. Furnishers' Response Times and Rates

Based on the information that the FTC and the Board reviewed, it appears that most disputes are processed in the statutory time frame, regardless of whether they are processed by e-OSCAR or by fax and mail. According to CDIA, e-OSCAR allows furnishers to prioritize all disputes to ensure that the most urgent ones are processed first and that all disputes can be processed within the time frames established by the FCRA.[142] As the time limit for responding to a dispute approaches, e-OSCAR notifies the furnisher of the impending deadline.[143] CDIA noted that, of the disputes that all three repositories sent through e-OSCAR in April 2004, furnishers responded within the following time periods:

- 54% within 0–7 days;
- 18% within 8–14 days;
- 22% within 15–30 days; and
- 6% did not respond within 30 days.[144]

CDIA also supplied statistics (*see* appendix D) showing the July 2004 response rates of furnishers that responded to one of the three repositories using e-OSCAR and furnishers that responded to the repository in paper form.[145] According to CDIA, as of day 10, 50.98% of the e-OSCAR furnishers had responded to this CRA regarding the disputes forwarded to them by the repository. At the same time, 24.33% of paper-based furnishers had responded. By day 20, 79.47% of e-OSCAR furnishers and 71.50% of paper-based furnishers had responded. By the end of the month, e-OSCAR furnishers had responded to 94% of the disputes from the repository, and paper-based furnishers had responded to 82%.

A number of furnishers reported that disputes received from CRAs by paper or by e-OSCAR are normally resolved within twenty days, and often within the first five days after receipt.[146] The Coalition to Implement the FACT

Act (Coalition) reported that its members meet the FCRA's thirty-day response requirement 100% of the time when using e-OSCAR.[147]

The consumer groups commented that the length of time CRAs and furnishers take to complete reinvestigations generally is not a problem, and that reinvestigations usually are finished very quickly through the e-OSCAR system.[148]

E. CRA Communicates Reinvestigation Results to Consumer

If a furnisher does not respond to the CRA within the 30-day period established by the FCRA, the CRA is required to treat the disputed information as unverifiable and delete the information.[149] TransUnion stated that if a response is not received within twenty-eight days, the information in dispute is automatically deleted from the consumer's credit file.[150]

Of the 18% of consumers in the GAO study who had disputed information in their files, 69% reported that the disputed information had been removed from their credit files. Another 23% reported that their disputed information had not been removed, and 7% said they did not know whether it had been removed.[151] Of those consumers in the survey who reported that information they disputed had been removed, approximately 72% said the information was not reinserted later, 13% reported that the information had been reinserted, and 15% did not know.[152]

CDIA provided the following data for the first five months of 2004, showing the resolution of disputes processed through the e-OSCAR system.[153]

Result of Dispute	% of Disputes
Data modified per data furnisher's instructions	53.64
Information verified as reported	22.37
Data deleted per data furnisher's direction	17.74
Data deleted due to furnisher not responding within the thirty-day period	6.27

We note that the percentage of consumers in the GAO survey who reported that disputed information had been removed from their file—69%—is similar to the percentage of consumers whose disputed information was either modified or deleted based on the furnisher's instructions—71.38%. According to CDIA, however, with respect to the "Data modified per data furnisher's instructions" category, the data may have been modified due to an update of information, rather than the data being found to be inaccurate as of the date reported.[154] With respect to the fourth category—data deleted due to the furnisher not responding within the thirty- day period—CDIA stated that it cannot be determined whether these data were accurate.[155]

TransUnion noted that it identified approximately 5% of disputes as "repeats," meaning that the repository recently processed the same dispute and the consumer has provided no new information.[156] In such cases, TransUnion may treat the dispute as frivolous and notify the consumer accordingly, without sending a dispute notice to the furnisher.[157]

F. Consumer Disputes Information Directly to Furnisher

In addition to disputes received from CRAs, furnishers also receive disputes directly from consumers about information reported to CRAs. As noted earlier, of the consumers in the GAO survey who said they disputed information in their credit files, 32% reported that they disputed with a CRA only, 29% reported that they disputed with the creditor only, and 30% reported that they disputed with both a CRA and the creditor.[158] Furnishers that submitted comments generally reported that they receive most of their disputes from CRAs.[159] As discussed above, until the new consumer-direct-dispute provision of the FACT Act takes effect, the FCRA does not specifically require that furnishers investigate disputes conveyed directly to them by consumers.[160] However, the FCRA does (1) prohibit furnishers that report regularly from reporting information they have determined is inaccurate and (2) require them to report corrected information.[161]

Some furnishers that commented reported that they provide or plan to provide a specific address or other information sufficient for consumers to initiate a dispute directly with them.[162] For example, Juniper Bank reported that it provides a specific address for direct disputes on all of its monthly billing statements.[163] Similarly, Wells Fargo commented that while some of its divisions and affiliates already do so, virtually all of them plan to begin providing addresses soon to consumers who want to dispute information directly.[164] Some furnishers do not provide a specific address dedicated to receiving disputes on information reported to CRAs, but instead provide general contact information that consumers can use to raise complaints and inquiries generally, including disputes on information provided to CRAs.[165] Furnishers that did not provide a specific address for reporting disputes directly provided various reasons for not doing so, including that (1) such disputes represent too small a percentage of the total inquiries and disputes received to justify establishing a specific address for such disputes; (2) a specific address would not be provided at a useful time; while the address would appear on initial disclosures or periodic statements, consumers generally learn of potential inaccuracies from receiving and reviewing consumer reports—not from the disclosures; and (3) the more appropriate address to publicly disclose is that of the three repositories.[166]

Whether or not a furnisher provides a specific address for receiving disputes directly from a consumer, most furnishers reported that they use a similar procedure for investigating direct disputes as they use for disputes received through a CRA,[167] including making any necessary corrections by sending the results of their investigations through e-OSCAR or in paper form.[168] Some furnishers commented that, upon receiving disputes directly from consumers, they compare information and documentation submitted by the consumers to information contained in their files.[169] In some cases, furnishers send letters to consumers notifying them that the information will be corrected.[170] Furnishers also report updating their own records to ensure that the erroneous information does not "re-pollute" the CRA's files when the furnisher sends its next monthly update.[171] If the information is found to be accurate, a letter may be sent to the consumer and reporting continues as before.[172] In general, the furnisher commenters stated that they investigate and attempt to resolve disputes directly from consumers as soon as possible, usually within one to twenty—and no more than thirty—days.[173]

Several furnishers reported that while most consumers provide sufficient information for the furnisher to investigate the consumer's dispute,[174] disputes received directly from consumers sometimes lack clarity as to the precise information disputed or fail to provide information sufficient to justify the dispute. According to the Coalition, for example, one of its members reported that 30% of all direct consumer disputes it receives fall into this category; another member that is a major credit grantor reported that 40% of its direct disputes contained insufficient information to conduct an investigation.[175] The type of information that is usually missing from consumers in direct disputes includes the consumer's full account number, Social Security number, date of birth, and address.[176] MBA noted that, on occasion, a consumer will refuse to send in a copy of his or her credit report. If the mortgage furnisher is given the authority by the CRA to view its tradeline as it appears in the CRA's database without impacting the consumer's credit score (i.e., as an inquiry), the mortgage furnisher will do so if this is relevant to the dispute.[177] Several furnishers commented that when relevant information is missing, the furnisher generally contacts the consumer by telephone or mail to request the necessary additional information.[178]

G. Commenters' Overall Views on the Dispute Process

The consumer groups and the credit reporting industry hold differing views on how well the current dispute process is working. The consumer groups maintain that the reinvestigation system in its current form is flawed because of what they regard as failures by both the CRAs and furnishers to conduct meaningful investigations of disputes.[179] As noted above, the consumer groups assert that CRAs typically do not provide furnishers with the documentation of the error that the consumer sent to the CRAs, that the CRAs generally do not review that documentation, and that the codes used by the CRAs to convey the nature of the dispute are too general and vague. The consumer groups also state that furnishers' investigations of disputed information are inadequate because they typically consist merely of verifying that their own records show that a debt exists.[180] They believe that CRAs and furnishers have little incentive to conduct thorough reinvestigations because such investigations are expensive and the relatively small number of lawsuits that CRAs and furnishers face for failing to conduct adequate investigations impose almost no economic cost.[181] According to the consumer groups, furnishers actually have an incentive to keep derogatory information in a consumer's credit file, "even if it is inaccurate … because the negative information limits the consumer's options to obtain other, less expensive debt, and is often the impetus to force a consumer to pay the furnisher even on an unjust claim."[182]

The consumer groups recommend that the current system be reformed to shift or counter these economic incentives. They suggest a role for lay advocates or independent third-party review in the reinvestigation system. They also recommend making statutory damages more readily available, so that CRAs and furnishers would take their duties more seriously.[183]

The consumer groups also suggest increasing the duties on furnishers as another option for improving the current system. These groups state that consumers currently have the impossible burden of proving that the disputed information is not correct to both furnishers and CRAs. They believe that the burden of proof should be shifted so that furnishers are required to rebut a consumer's specific disputes by providing documentation to the CRA that shows that the information furnished is correct. In particular, the consumer groups believe that furnishers should not be allowed simply to tell the CRA that the consumer is wrong and the original information was correct, and CRAs should not be allowed to accept such a report. Instead, the furnisher should be required to give the CRA the underlying information—copies of documents with original signatures to rebut a forgery claim, for example, or copies of the payment record to demonstrate that the claimed balance is correct. Then, the CRA should be required to evaluate the data and reach its own conclusions.[184]

The consumer groups believe that the dispute process should require, at a minimum, the following:

- CRAs to convey to furnishers the actual documents that support the consumer's dispute, with failure to do so being per se unreasonable;
- furnishers to reinvestigate, rather than merely verify, that the information appears in their records, including reviewing the actual documents provided by the consumer and, in appropriate circumstances, reviewing documents in the furnisher's possession or the possession of others;
- furnishers to respond specifically and in detail to the consumer's dispute and include enough material so that the CRA can evaluate the response and reach an independent conclusion;
- CRAs to review and evaluate furnishers' responses; and
- CRAs to establish an appeals process that involves a telephone conference between the consumer and a CRA employee who has the consumer's dispute and all the documentation provided by the furnisher and the consumer.[185]

Approximately 100 consumers provided comments for this report, generally expressing a variety of problems they encountered in resolving their disputes.[186] For the most part, these individual accounts parallel the concerns raised by the consumer groups.

The California Association of Realtors recommended that sufficient financial penalties be imposed for violations of the FCRA to allow the FTC to protect the integrity of credit reports and to create the proper incentives for creditors and CRAs to comply.[187] The Mortgage Bankers Association recommended that the e-OSCAR system be changed to permit furnishers to submit comments to CRAs when they return ACDVs.[188]

Most industry commenters—furnishers and their trade groups and the repositories and their trade group—asserted that while there is still room for improvement, the current dispute process generally is working well, and that legislative and regulatory changes would not be appropriate at this time.[189] Visa U.S.A. Inc. (Visa), a membership organization composed of financial institutions, gave several reasons it believes that the current system is effective in removing inaccuracies.[190] First, Visa argued, financial institutions have strong incentives to investigate disputed information adequately in order to maintain good relationships with their customers. Visa also pointed out that, in providing information to CRAs, financial institutions typically report information as it appears that month in the institution's own records. According to Visa, financial institutions have strong incentives to ensure that their own records are accurate, because the records are essential for the institution's own collection activities and other important business purposes, for making reports to their federal and state bank regulatory agencies, and, where applicable, for making securities filings.

Visa warned that any additional requirements and liability on furnishers would have a negative impact on the nationwide credit reporting and credit granting systems.[191] According to Visa, the more requirements imposed on, and the more liability risks incurred by, furnishers, the less likely it is they will continue to furnish information to CRAs. Visa noted that, should this occur, the entire nationwide credit system would suffer. A reduction in the supply of credit information, Visa argued, would increase the risks associated with extending credit because creditors would be required to make credit decisions on less complete information. The increased risk would be reflected in an increase in the costs consumers must pay for credit. Visa contended that this increased risk also would have an anticompetitive impact on financial institutions, where smaller lenders are less able to absorb the cost of this increased risk than larger lenders. Thus, smaller lenders could find it difficult to price their products to compete with larger lenders. Visa also warned that a shortage of consumer report information would decrease competition by making it difficult for creditors to serve consumers across the country through national credit programs. In addition, the types and amounts of credit available to consumers could be restricted.

Visa and Juniper also warned that potential changes in the dispute process (such as shorter time frames to investigate disputes) could impact industry's fraud prevention efforts.[192] Several commenters indicated that the financial industry continues to be plagued by "debt elimination" schemes and abuses by some borrowers and credit repair organizations that initiate disputes designed to overwhelm the dispute system, forcing removal of accurate, but unfavorable, information.[193] Visa warned that any changes to shorten the time periods to investigate and correct consumer report information would benefit credit repair organizations by forcing the deletion of correct, but unfavorable, information that cannot be verified in a shorter period.[194] According to Visa, this would lead to less accurate consumer report files and greater risk for creditors who rely on consumer reports to underwrite credit requests. Juniper argued that any new proposals need to be examined to ensure that they are not providing another avenue for individuals to avoid legitimate debt.[195]

Other commenters indicated that, given the FACT Act provisions, further legislative and regulatory actions are not needed at this time. The Coalition and MBNA report that to the extent problems have occurred, they almost entirely relate to cases of identity theft.[196] These commenters point out that the FACT Act contains a number of key provisions to deal with problems of identity theft and should be fully implemented before it is possible to determine whether there are any remaining reinvestigation issues. According to TransUnion, the improvements made through the 1996 FCRA amendments, combined with the as-yet unknown impact of the FACT Act's amendments concerning accuracy, reinvestigations, and the processing of consumer disputes by furnishers and resellers, make further statutory or regulatory changes inadvisable at this time.[197]

V. FCRA ENFORCEMENT

The FTC and the federal financial regulators are responsible for enforcing the FCRA.[198] The FTC's jurisdiction extends to all CRAs and other persons not specifically committed to another agency's jurisdiction.[199] The FTC does not formally examine its regulated entities for compliance with the FCRA, but rather conducts selected law enforcement investigations and brings legal actions against violators. The FTC has brought a number of actions against CRAs[200] and furnishers[201] for violations of the FCRA's dispute and accuracy provisions.

Financial institutions regulated by the federal financial regulators generally are subject to the FCRA dispute provisions primarily due to their role as furnishers of information to CRAs. The federal financial regulators examine these institutions for compliance with the FCRA, including the FCRA dispute provisions. The federal financial regulators have FCRA examination procedures that each decides how to implement. For example, the Federal

Reserve System implements these procedures as part of routine consumer compliance examinations. A Federal Reserve Bank examiner considers the bank's processes for complying with the FCRA accuracy and dispute provisions when performing a preliminary risk assessment of the bank and setting the scope of the consumer compliance examination, and applies the FCRA examination procedures, as appropriate.

While state-chartered banks make up only a portion of the furnishers, for this study, bank examiners for the Federal Reserve and Federal Deposit Insurance Corporation (FDIC) looked at violations by state-chartered banks of the dispute provisions governing furnishers and found an insignificant number of violations.[202] These two federal financial regulators, along with the OCC, also surveyed their complaint databases for this study to determine the number and types of consumer complaints regarding disputed consumer file information.[203] Both the Board and the OCC provided data from 2000 to 2004; the FDIC provided data from 2002 to 2004. While some consumers complained that inaccurate or incomplete information remained in their files, or that a furnisher failed to conduct or complete an investigation to the consumers' satisfaction, in general, the data did not indicate a large number of complaints regarding failures by furnishers to properly reinvestigate information disputed by consumers.

Under section 611(e), the FTC is required to transmit to the repositories complaints from consumers who appear to have disputed the completeness or accuracy of their files with one or more repositories or otherwise utilized their dispute rights under FCRA section 611(a). Section 611(e) also requires that the repositories review the complaints, report to the FTC on the results of their review, and maintain sufficient records to show compliance.

To implement section 611(e), the FTC entered into a complaint-referral program with the three repositories and a number of affiliate CRAs that store their data in the repositories' databases.[204]

Under the program, the FTC refers to the repositories and the affiliates' complaints that it receives from consumers who report that their disputes about accuracy or completeness have not been resolved to their satisfaction.

The FTC makes no determination about the merits of the complaints. The CRAs review the complaints to ensure that they have complied with the applicable provisions of the FCRA and periodically provide reports to the FTC on the disposition of a sample of the complaints. The program does not limit the FTC's ability to pursue law violations under the FCRA.

Because the data that the FTC has obtained through the complaint-referral program to date are insufficient to provide probative evidence of the functioning of the dispute resolution process, this report contains no findings on that issue.

CONCLUSION

In compliance with FACT Act section 313(b), the FTC and the Board have studied the FCRA dispute process by reviewing information from a number of sources. There is general consensus that CRAs and furnishers usually are conducting their investigations within the thirty- day period set forth in FCRA section 611(a)(1).

However, many commenters held differing views on the subject of FCRA compliance by CRAs and furnishers. Consumer groups that commented, for example, assert that CRAs do not convey "all relevant information" to furnishers, and that both CRAs and furnishers typically fail to conduct meaningful investigations. These groups recommend that the current system be reformed to induce CRAs and furnishers to take their duties to investigate disputes seriously.

Most industry commenters, however, maintain that, while there is room for improvement, the current dispute process generally is working well and additional legislative and regulatory changes are not advisable at this time. Courts also have reached different conclusions on the subject of CRA and furnisher compliance, generally applying a reasonableness standard to CRA and furnisher investigations and then determining whether the investigation at issue was reasonable based on the facts of each case.[205]

With respect to the FCRA's requirement that CRAs forward to the furnisher "all relevant information," it appears that CRAs generally do not convey to furnishers documents that some consumers give CRAs in connection with their disputes.

By itself, however, this does not mean that CRAs fail to convey "all relevant information" to furnishers. It is unclear how often consumers submit documents along with their disputes, or how often these documents contain relevant information.

When consumers do submit documents, the CRAs summarize the information in a numeric code supplemented, in some instances, by a narrative in a free-form field. Although this process may be sufficient in most cases to resolve the dispute properly, in certain situations, the failure to convey the actual documents may lead to incorrect outcomes.

The information that the FTC and the Board have obtained on this subject is inconclusive as to the prevalence of this result.

Likewise, the question of whether CRAs and furnishers generally are conducting investigations that comply with the FCRA cannot be resolved definitively. Although some consumers ultimately file a dispute statement regarding information that has not been corrected or deleted after reinvestigation, it is not clear whether these disputes reflect a failure to comply with the FCRA reinvestigation procedures or simply consumer dissatisfaction with the results of the reinvestigations, despite CRA and furnisher compliance. Similarly, evidence regarding compliance by the consumer reporting industry is inconclusive.

The FTC and the Board agree with courts holding that (1) CRA and furnisher investigations must be reasonable and (2) whether an investigation is reasonable depends on the facts in each case.

FACT Act section 313(b)(4) requires that the FTC and the Board include in this report any legislative or administrative recommendations for improvements to the dispute process that the agencies jointly determine to be appropriate. The agencies recommend that no legislative action be taken at this time, in large part because the agencies believe such action would be premature. The FACT Act imposes a number of new requirements on CRAs and furnishers that should enhance the consumer dispute process and improve accuracy, including measures to reduce identity theft and new requirements on furnishers.[206] Many of these requirements are still being implemented, and their effects on the dispute process have yet to be seen. The FTC and the Board believe that the FACT Act requirements should be given time to take effect before legislators and regulators consider making additional changes to the dispute process. This is particularly important given the voluntary nature of the reporting system and the uncertainty of how additional requirements and burdens would affect that system. As additional information becomes available, the agencies will reassess the need for administrative actions. With respect to the "all relevant information" issue, there may be a number of ways to address the concerns that have been expressed about the process, ranging from different or more specific codes, to greater use of the narrative field, to better training of personnel who do the coding, to the scanning or other conveyance of documents to furnishers. The costs and benefits of each of these steps cannot be determined on the basis of the current record. The FTC and the Board intend to explore further these issues and possible solutions with the CRAs, furnishers, consumer advocates, and other interested parties, and, if appropriate, will make recommendations for action.

Appendix A. Table of Names and Acronyms

ABA	American Bankers Association
ACB	Associated Credit Bureaus
ACDV	Automated Consumer Dispute Verification
AUD	Automated Universal Data
BB&T	Branch Banking and Trust Company
BECU	Boeing Employees' Credit Union
Board	Board of Governors of the Federal Reserve System
CDIA	Consumer Data Industry Association
CDV	Consumer Dispute Verification
Coalition	The Coalition to Implement the FACT Act
Consumer Groups	National Consumer Law Center, Consumer Federation of America, Consumers Union, Electronic Privacy Clearinghouse, and U.S. Public Interest Research Group
CRA	Consumer Reporting Agency
e-OSCAR	Online Solution for Complete and Accurate Reporting
FACT Act	Fair and Accurate Credit Transactions Act of 2003
FCRA	Fair Credit Reporting Act
FDIC	Federal Deposit Insurance Corporation
Federal Financial Regulators	The Board, Federal Deposit Insurance Corporation, National Credit Union Administration, Office of the Comptroller of the Currency, and Office of Thrift Supervision.
FTC	Federal Trade Commission
GAO	Government Accountability Office
Juniper	Juniper Bank
MBA	Mortgage Bankers Association
MBNA	MBNA America Bank
Metro/Metro 2	Standard layouts for furnishers to report information to consumer reporting agencies
NAMB	National Association of Mortgage Brokers
NCRA	National Credit Reporting Association
OCC	Office of the Comptroller of the Currency
UDF	Universal Data Form
Visa	Visa U.S.A. Inc.
Wells Fargo	Wells Fargo & Company
Zions	Zions Bancorporation
1996 FCRA	The FCRA as amended in 1996 and 1999 but before the FACT Act amendments in December 2003

Appendix B. Sample Automated Consumer Dispute Verification Form[207]

Return this dispute response to:

ICRA - exp affiliated

123 Street New Town, NY 12603–

FAX # -

Date : 05-19-2006

Control # 9070605040

Account Number 37012345678

DNR Date 05-19-2006

Subscriber Code DF Credit/dfcreditexp

Response Date 05-19-2006

Please check the SAME box for each identification Item appearing on the CDV which is identical to your records;or provide differing information in the shaded area.

		SAME		
Name/Gen Code	John Q Consumer / —	☐	**Name/Gen Code**	- Quentin - / ---
Address	123 Main St, atlanta GA 30328–	☑	**Address**	-.----
Prev Name/Prev Gen Code	---/—	☐	**Prev Name/Prev Gen Code**	---/—
Prev Address	8946 S Water St, Chicago IL 60601–	☐	**Prev Address**	525 W Belmont St, Chicago IL 60657--
SSN	909122242	☑	**SSN**	-
DOB	04-15-1965	☑	**DOB**	-
Telephone Number	4045251212	☐	**Telephone Number**	4048325454
2nd Prev Addr	-, -- —			

Consumer States/Comments:
Dispute Code 1: 24:Claims account closed by consumer. Verify Compliance Condition Code, Account Status, Date Closed, and Payment Rating.
Dispute Code 2:
FCRA Relevant Information: Account paid in full and closed on 5/4/06. Check number 7682

Please write clearly and report changed information in the shaded box directly below where it is currently reported.

Verified as Reported ☐ **Change Data as Shown** ☑ **Delete Account** ☐ **Delete due to Fraud** ☐

Acct Status	Pay Rate	MOP	Cond/Cumm Status	Date Opened	Balance	Amt Past Due	High Cr/Org	Credit Lmit	Org Chg Off Amt
11	0	-	-	02-05-1999	14386	-	68000	-	-
13	0			-	0	0	-	-	-

Acct Type	Portf Type	Terms Dur	Freq	Date of Account Information	Date Closed	Date of Last Pymnt	Sch Pymnt	ECOA	Status Date (EXP only)	FCRA DOFD
6D	I	-	-	04-15-2006	-	04-15-2006	734	1	-	-
-	-	-	-	05-19-2006	05-09-2006	05-09-2006	-	-	-	-

CCC	SCC	CII	Orig Cr Name	Orig Cr Class	Spec Pymnt Ind	Deferred Start Date	Balloon Date	Balloon Amt
-	-	-	-	-	-	-	-	-
-	-	-	-	-	-	-	-	-

Accounts History

0	0	0	0	0	0	0	0	0	0	1	0	0	0	0	0	0	1	0	0	0	0	0	0
0	0	0	0	0	0	1	0	0	0	0	0	0	0	0	0	0	0	0	0	0	0	0	0
0	0	0	0	0	1	0	0	0	0	0	0	0	0	0	0	0	0	0	0	0	0	0	0
0	0	1	0	0	0	0	0	0	0	0	0												
0	0	0	0	0	0	0	0	0	0	0	1	0	0	0	0	0	1	0	0	0	0	0	0
0	0	0	0	0	0	1	0	0	0	0	0	0	0	0	0	0	0	0	0	0	0	0	0
0	0	0	0	0	0	1	0	0	0	0	0	0	0	0	0	0	0	0	0	0	0	0	0
0	0	1	0	0	0	0	0	0	0	0	0												

Agency ID	Sec Mktg Agency Acct #	Mortgage ID
-	-	-
-	-	-
Actual Pymnt	**Portfolio Indicator**	**Prchsd from/Sold to**
980	-	-
-	—	-

Remarks : -

DF Contact # : 9723903912

Authorized Name ____________________ Tel # ____________________

When you sign this form, you certify that you have verified the accuracy of the entire item in compliance with all legal requirements, and your computer and/or manual records will be adjusted to reflect changes noted above.

Appendix C. Frequency of Credit Account Disputes in Federal Reserve Board Study of Data from One Repository as of June 30, 2003[208]

Table 1. Frequency of pending disputes, by number of accounts affected

	Credit card	Mortgage	Auto	Other	All types
No dispute	99.63%	99.98%	100%	99.96%	99.82%
Pending dispute	0.37%	0.02%	0	0.04%	0.18%
Number of accounts of this type	666,152	88,014	7,176	719,140	1,480,482

Table 2. Share of pending disputes, by type of credit

	Credit card	Mortgage	Auto	Other
Pending dispute	89.86%	0.73%	0.00%	9.41%

Table 3. Distribution of pending disputes based on status of account

	Credit card	Mortgage	Auto	Other	All types
Pending disputes on open accounts	87.41%	89.47%	N/A	66.15%	85.39%
Pending disputes on closed accounts	12.59%	10.53%	N/A	33.85%	14.61%

Appendix D. Response Rates of Furnishers Responding to One Repository through E-OSCAR and Furnishers Responding in Paper Form (July 2004)[209]

Response Time (# Days)	E-Oscar: Monthly accumulated % of responses to all disputes	Paper: Monthly accumulated % of responses to all disputes
0		
1		
2	4.96%	3.08%
3	12.46%	6.39%
4	19.12%	8.27%
5	26.71%	9.74%
6	32.29%	12.19%
7	38.89%	16.60%
8	44.90%	19.20%
9	48.40%	21.93%
10	50.98%	24.33%
11	54.13%	27.95%
12	57.15%	31.32%
13	59.69%	36.78%
14	62.43%	44.18%
15	65.33%	51.14%
16	68.15%	57.02%
17	71.05%	61.25%
18	74.64%	64.43%
19	78.06%	68.08%
20	79.47%	71.50%
21	80.82%	74.80%
22	82.56%	77.12%
23	84.35%	78.29%
24	85.95%	79.32%
25	88.09%	80.13%
26	89.98%	80.85%
27	92.24%	81.60%
28	94.00%	82.00%

APPENDIX E. THE FCRA AFTER THE FACT ACT

In the FACT Act amendments, Congress made three changes to the core dispute duties of CRAs. The provision stating that CRAs "shall reinvestigate" information that consumers dispute was amended to require CRAs to "conduct a reasonable reinvestigation to determine whether the disputed information is inaccurate."[210] In addition, a CRA that learns during a reinvestigation that information disputed by a consumer is inaccurate, incomplete, or cannot be verified, now must notify the furnisher that the information has been modified or deleted from the CRA's file on the consumer.[211] Finally, the FACT Act amendments give CRAs forty-five days to reinvestigate a dispute from a consumer that is made following the consumer's receipt of a free annual file disclosure under the Act's new free file disclosure provisions.[212]

The FACT Act substantially changed the dispute duties for resellers.[213] Because resellers are CRAs, the FCRA, prior to the FACT Act, required them to carry out all of the CRA dispute duties described in section II.C of the attached report. A new provision added by the FACT Act, however, changed those duties. If a consumer disputes directly to a reseller the completeness or accuracy of an item in a consumer report issued by the reseller, the reseller must, within five business days of receiving notice of the dispute, and free of charge, do the following:[214]

- determine whether the item is incomplete or inaccurate because of an act or omission of the reseller; and
- if the reseller determines that the item is incomplete or inaccurate because of an act of the reseller, not less than 20 days after receiving the notice, correct the information in the consumer report or delete it; or
- if the reseller determines that the item is not incomplete or inaccurate because of an act or omission of the reseller, convey the notice of dispute, together with all relevant information provided by the consumer, to each CRA that provided the disputed item to the reseller ("source CRA").

Another FACT Act provision requires a source CRA to reinvestigate a dispute conveyed by a reseller.[215] Upon completion of its reinvestigation, the source CRA must provide to the reseller a written notice stating the results of the reinvestigation.[216] The reseller must immediately reconvey the notice to the consumer.[217]

The FACT Act also amended the FCRA with respect to furnishers' dispute duties in several ways. Under one of the amendments, the FTC and the federal financial regulators are required to issue joint regulations that will identify the circumstances under which a furnisher must investigate a dispute made directly by a consumer to the furnisher. In prescribing the regulations, the agencies must weigh several factors, including the benefits to consumers versus the costs to furnishers and the credit reporting system. In those circumstances identified in the rules, the rules must provide that, when a consumer submits a proper notice of dispute to a furnisher, the furnisher must conduct an investigation of the disputed information; review all relevant information provided by the consumer with the notice; complete the investigation within thirty days (or forty-five days, if the consumer provides additional relevant information during the thirty-day period); and, if the investigation finds that the disputed item was reported inaccurately, promptly provide corrections to each CRA to which the information was furnished.[218] These provisions do not apply if the dispute is frivolous or irrelevant or comes from a credit repair organization.

The FACT Act also provides that, in disputes received through a CRA, if an item of information disputed by a consumer is found to be inaccurate or incomplete or cannot be verified after the furnisher completes the investigation, the furnisher must promptly delete, modify, or permanently block the reporting of that information as appropriate based on the results of the investigation.[219] In addition, the FACT Act provides that furnishers must establish reasonable procedures to avoid re-furnishing to CRAs information after (1) a CRA notifies the furnisher that the CRA has blocked the information because it might be the result of identity theft or (2) the consumer submits an identity theft report stating that the information resulted from identity theft.[220]

Prior to the FACT Act, furnishers could not furnish information about a consumer to a CRA if the furnisher knew or consciously avoided knowing that the information was inaccurate.[221] Under the FACT Act, the standard is now "knows or has reasonable cause to believe that the information is inaccurate."[222] The term "reasonable cause to believe that the information is inaccurate" is defined as "having specific knowledge, other than solely allegations by the consumer, that would cause a reasonable person to have substantial doubts about the accuracy of the information."[223]

The FACT Act amendments require a financial institution that furnishes negative information about a consumer to a nationwide CRA to notify the consumer in writing.[224] In addition, the amendments require federal financial regulators and the FTC to promulgate guidelines and regulations dealing with the accuracy and integrity of information that furnishers provide to CRAs.[225]

End Notes

[1] Pub. L. 108–159, 117 Stat. 1952. Although the FACT Act makes many improvements to the dispute process, the Act's provisions are still in the initial stages of implementation. Consequently, this report is based solely on compliance with the pre–FACT Act FCRA.

[2] FCRA section 611(e), also enacted as part of the FACT Act, requires that the FTC transmit to the three nationwide consumer reporting agencies ("repositories")—Equifax Information Services, LLC (Equifax), Experian Information Solutions, Inc. (Experian), and TransUnion LLC (TransUnion)—complaints from consumers who appear to have disputed the completeness or accuracy of their files with one or more repositories or otherwise exercised their dispute rights under FCRA section 611(a). FCRA section 611(e) also requires that the repositories review the complaints, report to the FTC on the results of their review, and maintain records sufficient to show compliance.

[3] Request for Information for Study on Investigations of Disputed Consumer Information Reported to Consumer Reporting Agencies, 69 Fed. Reg. 48,494 (Aug. 10, 2004).

[4] Approximately 100 consumers submitted comments in response to the Board's Federal Register notice.

[5] The National Consumer Law Center, Consumer Federation of America, Consumers Union, Electronic Privacy Clearinghouse, and U.S. Public Interest Research Group ("consumer groups") submitted a joint comment.

[6] Commenters that provided information for this report on behalf of furnishers include the Ford County State Bank (Ford County Bank), Juniper Bank (Juniper), Zions Bancorporation (Zions), Wells Fargo & Company (Wells Fargo), Boeing Employees Credit Union (BECU), Branch Banking and Trust Company (BB&T), MBNA America Bank (MBNA), Visa U.S.A. Inc. (Visa), American Bankers Association (ABA), Mortgage Bankers Association (MBA), and Coalition to Implement the FACT Act (Coalition). The Coalition represents an array of financial services companies that are furnishers and/or users of consumer credit information. Comment of Coalition, at 1.

[7] For this report, both Equifax and TransUnion submitted comment letters, as did the National Credit Reporting Association (NCRA), a trade association that represents resellers of consumer reports, and the Consumer Data Industry Association (CDIA). Formerly known as Associated Credit Bureaus, Inc., CDIA represents many of the nation's largest CRAs, including Equifax, Experian, and TransUnion. Comment of CDIA, at 1 n.1.

[8] The following trade associations also submitted comments: the National Association of Realtors, California Association of Realtors, National Association of Mortgage Brokers (NAMB), and Florida Association of Mortgage Brokers.

[9] This report uses the term "federal financial regulators" to refer collectively to the following entities: the Board, Federal Deposit Insurance Corporation (FDIC), National Credit Union Administration (NCUA), Office of the Comptroller of the Currency (OCC), and Office of Thrift Supervision (OTS).

[10] When the FCRA was enacted in 1970, the credit reporting industry consisted of more than 2,500 independent local and regional credit bureaus across the country. *Written Statement of John A. Ford, Chief Privacy Officer, Equifax Inc.: Hearing Before the House Committee on Financial Institutions and Consumer Credit*, 108th Cong. (June 4, 2003) [hereinafter Statement of John A. Ford], at 5. Over time, however, most of these credit bureaus were consolidated into the three existing repositories. For a detailed discussion of the history and development of the consumer reporting system, *see* Robert M. Hunt, *A Century of*

Consumer Credit Reporting in America (Federal Reserve Bank of Philadelphia Working Paper No. 05-13, June 2005).

[11] *See* Robert B. Avery, Paul S. Calem & Glenn B. Canner, *Credit Report Accuracy and Access to Credit, Federal Reserve Bulletin* (Summer 2004) [hereinafter 2004 FRB Study], at 298.

[12] Comment of CDIA, at 10.

[13] 2004 FRB Study, *supra* note 11, at 298.

[14] *Id.*

[15] Communication from CDIA to the Division of Financial Practices, Federal Trade Commission (Jan. 7, 2005) (on file with the Division of Privacy & Identity Protection) [hereinafter CDIA Communication 01/07/05].

[16] FCRA section 603(f) defines "consumer reporting agency" as "any person which, for monetary fees, dues, or on a cooperative nonprofit basis, regularly engages in whole or in part in the practice of assembling or evaluating consumer credit information or other information on consumers for the purpose of furnishing consumer reports to third parties, and which uses any means or facility of interstate commerce for the purpose of preparing or furnishing consumer reports."

[17] In the FTC's Free Annual File Disclosure Rule, these agencies are termed "associated consumer reporting agencies." 16 C.F.R. § 610.1(b)(2). Although each of these arrangements is unique, the repository with which such an agency is associated typically has the right to sell the agency's data to the repository's customers.

[18] The CRAs in this category that operate on a nationwide basis are referred to as "nationwide specialty consumer reporting agencies." *See* FCRA § 603(w).

[19] All entities that procure consumer reports for purposes of reselling them must comply with FCRA section 607(e), which requires that these entities take certain steps before reselling the reports. The FACT Act, however, added special provisions with respect to the dispute duties of certain of these entities. The special provisions apply only to "resellers." A reseller is defined as

> consumer reporting agency that (1) assembles and merges information contained in the database of another consumer reporting agency or multiple consumer reporting agencies concerning any consumer for purposes of furnishing such information to any third party, to the extent of such activities; and (2) does not maintain a database of the assembled or merged information from which new consumer reports are produced.

FCRA § 603(u). Some CRAs that resell repository information merely forward, or "pass through," the information. These entities fall outside the FCRA section 603(u) definition of "reseller," because they do not "assemble and merge" the information, but they still must comply with FCRA section 607(e).

[20] Comment of CDIA, at 4, 10 n.8.

[21] Comment of CDIA, at 4.

[22] *See* Robert B. Avery, Paul S. Calem, Glenn B. Canner & Raphael W. Bostic, *An Overview of Consumer Data and Credit Reporting, Federal Reserve Bulletin* (Feb. 2003) [hereinafter 2003 FRB Study], at 49, 50; Comment of NAMB, at 2; Comment of Equifax, at 5.

[23] *See* 2003 FRB Study, *supra* note 22, at 48; Statement of John A. Ford, *supra* note 10, at 8–9. In addition to "credit reports," repositories also produce "credit scores," consumer reports that summarize a consumer's credit history in a number, or "score." For a fuller discussion of consumer reports and their uses in consumer transactions, *see* Federal Trade Commission, *Report to Congress Under Sections 318 and 319 of the Fair and Accurate Credit Transactions Act of 2003* (Dec. 2004) [hereinafter 2004 FTC Report], at 6–11.

[24] For furnishers that report to more than one repository, the standardized formats, known as Metro and Metro 2, ensure that the bits of information from these furnishers—e.g., last name, first name, address, and current balance—are received in the same data fields in the databases of any repositories to which the furnisher reports. *See infra* section III for a discussion of Metro and Metro 2.

[25] *See, e.g.*, Comment of Coalition, at page 3 of Coalition's attachment; Comment of NAMB, at 2; Comment of CDIA, at 4.

[26] National Consumer Law Center, *Fair Credit Reporting* (5th ed. & Supp. 2005) [hereinafter NCLC Treatise], at 55.

[27] 2003 FRB Study, *supra* note 22, at 51 n.11.

[28] *Id.*; *The Accuracy of Credit Report Information and the Fair Credit Reporting Act: Hearing Before the Senate Committee on Banking, Housing, and Urban Affairs*, 108th Cong. (July 10, 2003) (statement of Stuart K. Pratt, CDIA) [hereinafter Statement of Stuart K. Pratt], at 5.

[29] FCRA § 611(a)(1)(A). If a consumer transmits information relevant to the reinvestigation during the thirty-day period, the CRA has fifteen additional days to complete the reinvestigation. FCRA § 611(a)(1)(B). The FCRA uses the term "reinvestigation" when referring to reviews of disputed items conducted by CRAs and the term "investigation" when referring to reviews conducted by furnishers. *Compare* FCRA § 611(a) *with* FCRA § 623(b).

[30] FCRA § 611(a)(4).

[31] FCRA § 611(a)(2).

[32] FCRA § 623(b). The FCRA also imposes other duties on furnishers, a number of which are described in appendix E of this report.

[33] FCRA § 611(a)(5)(A). FCRA section 611(a) as originally enacted in 1970 required CRAs to delete information found to be inaccurate or unverifiable, but a 1996 amendment gave CRAs the choice of either deleting the information or modifying it.

[34] FCRA § 611(a)(6).

[35] Appendix E contains a more detailed discussion of the FACT Act changes to the FCRA. Other laws, such as the Fair Credit Billing Act, Electronic Fund Transfer Act, Real Estate Settlement Procedures Act, Equal Credit Opportunity Act, and Servicemembers Civil Relief Act, also contain requirements with respect to disputes or the furnishing of information. This report addresses only those requirements in the FCRA.

[36] *See* FCRA § 623(e), added by FACT Act § 312. In March 2006 the agencies published an Advance Notice of Proposed Rulemaking. 71 Fed. Reg. 14,419 (March 22, 2006).

[37] *See* FCRA § 623(a)(8), added by FACT Act § 312.

[38] FCRA § 623(b)(1)(E), added by FACT Act § 314.

[39] FCRA § 623(a)(7), added by FACT Act § 217. The Board issued two model notices that financial institutions may use to comply with this requirement. One may be used if the institution provides the notice prior to furnishing negative information to a nationwide CRA. The other may be used if the institution provides the notice after furnishing the negative information. 12 C.F.R. pt. 222 app. B.

[40] Comment of CDIA, at 10. Some furnishers report to CRAs by contracting with other companies to report on their behalf. Comment of Coalition, at page 1 of Coalition's attachment.

[41] Comment of TransUnion, at 3. *See also* Comment of Wells Fargo, at 1.

[42] FCRA § 623(a)(4). The furnisher must include this notice with the information it regularly furnishes to the CRA for the period in which the account is closed. *Id.* Furnishers that commented on this issue indicated that they report the closure in their next regularly scheduled report to the CRA, as required by law. Comment of BECU, at 3; Comment of Wells Fargo, at 4; Comment of Juniper, at 3; Comment of MBA, at 9; Comment of ABA, at 3; Comment of Zions, at 4; Comment of BB&T, at 5. However, the National Association of Mortgage Brokers stated that instead of reporting that an account is closed, some creditors simply stop sending updates on the account to CRAs. Comment of NAMB, at 7.

[43] FCRA § 623(a)(5). Some commenters stated that with respect to accounts that have been placed for collection or charged off, they report the date of the first delinquency with their regular monthly update to the CRAs. Comment of MBA, at 8; Comment of Ford County Bank, at 1; Comment of BECU, at 3; Comment of Wells Fargo, at 4; Comment of Zions, at

3–4; Comment of Juniper, at 3. NAMB was concerned that, in some cases, as a collection or charged-off account is sold and resold, a new date is attached to the account by each new furnisher, so it appears that the delinquency is more recent than it really is. Comment of NAMB, at 6. The practice described by NAMB likely would violate the FCRA. As noted above, the FCRA requires a furnisher that reports information to a CRA regarding a delinquent account being placed for collection, charged to profit or loss, or subjected to any similar action to notify the CRA of the month and year of the commencement of the delinquency that immediately preceded the action (often referred to as the "date of delinquency"), not later than ninety days after furnishing the information to the CRA. FCRA § 623(a)(5). No matter how many times a delinquent account is sold and resold, its date of delinquency should remain the same.

[44] Comment of MBA, at 2. In addition, MBA commented that mortgage furnishers are not allowed to report certain negative information. For example, Freddie Mac and Fannie Mae require forbearances on mortgages to be reported as military indulgences if the borrower is a service member on active duty and eligible for relief under the Servicemembers Civil Relief Act. Comment of MBA, at 5.

[45] Comment of CDIA, at 4. The ABA reported that only a small percentage of the very smallest institutions report only negative information. Comment of ABA, at 2.

[46] Comment of BB&T, at 1. Many banks in the Coalition's survey of twenty community banks stated that they do not report information on commercial loans and a variety of other loans such as agricultural loans, real estate loans, and overdraft- protection closed-end loans. Comment of Coalition, at page 2 of Coalition's attachment. A state member bank explained that in the course of a bank examination, it reports on all its mortgage and consumer loan products, but not on its commercial loans, as the commercial loan relationships are supported with cash generated from operating income and real estate investments.

[47] Comment of CDIA, at 4. Many creditors obtain lists of consumers from CRAs for the purpose of making "firm offers of credit" (often referred to as "prescreened offers"). The FCRA permits creditors to obtain these consumer lists under FCRA section 604(c) unless a consumer opts out of receiving such offers. By refraining from reporting positive data on their best customers, banks and other creditors can keep competitors from "cherry picking" those customers through prescreened offers.

[48] Comment of CDIA, at 4; Comment of NAMB, at 2.

[49] *See, e.g.*, Cal. Pub. Util. Code § 2891(a) (2004).

[50] Comment of Equifax, at 5.

[51] Comment of CDIA, at 4; Comment of TransUnion, at 4; Comment of Equifax, at 5; Comment of BECU, at 1; Comment of Coalition, at page 3 of Coalition's attachment.

[52] Commenters reported on the policies and procedures implemented to ensure compliance with the FCRA and the periodic auditing performed to ensure that information reported is accurate. *See* Comment of MBA, at 7–8; Comment of Coalition, at 4; Comment of MBNA, at 5; Comment of ABA, at 3; Comment of Wells Fargo, at 3; Comment of Juniper, at 2; Comment of BB&T, at 4; Comment of BECU, at 2. In addition, BECU reviews annual audits from each CRA to ensure that the CRAs are accurately recording information reported by BECU. Comment of BECU, at 2. Similarly, the Coalition reported that one of its members that performed such a review found that the CRA accurately recorded the reported information more than 99.7% of the time. *See* Comment of Coalition, at 4.

[53] Comment of CDIA, at 10.

[54] *Id.* Both Metro and Metro 2 are maintained by an industry committee of employees from each of the three repositories. *Id.*

[55] Communication from CDIA to the Division of Financial Practices, Federal Trade Commission (Jan. 12, 2005) (on file with the Division of Privacy & Identity Protection) [hereinafter CDIA Communication 01/12/05], at 1.

[56] CDIA, *Credit Reporting Resource Guide* (2003) [hereinafter CDIA Resource Guide], at 2-1.

[57] General Accounting Office, Report No. GAO-03-1036T, *Consumer Credit: Limited Information Exists on the Extent of Credit Report Errors and Their Implications for Consumers* (July 2003), at 12.

[58] CDIA Communication 01/12/05, *supra* note 55, at 2.

[59] Comment of CDIA, at 4.

[60] NCLC Treatise, *supra* note 26, at 55.

[61] *Id.* at 55–56.

[62] Until new FACT Act rules under FCRA § 623(a)(8) take effect, the FCRA does not specifically require that furnishers investigate disputes conveyed directly to them by consumers. Even before the rules take effect, however, the FCRA prohibits furnishers that report regularly from reporting information they have determined is inaccurate, and requires them to report corrected information. FCRA § 623(a)(2).

[63] Government Accountability Office, Report No. GAO-05-223, *Credit Reporting Literacy: Consumers Understand the Basics but Could Benefit From Targeted Educational Efforts* (March 2005) [hereinafter 2005 GAO Report], at 3, 20.

[64] *Id.* at 20–21, 64.

[65] CDIA Communication 01/07/05, *supra* note 15. In many cases, a single consumer may have received disclosures from multiple CRAs. Therefore it is difficult to compare CDIA's estimate of file disclosures to the GAO's estimate of the number of reports ordered by consumers.

[66] FCRA § 609(c)(2)(B).

[67] 2005 GAO Report, *supra* note 63, at 21, 64–65. Consumers in many circumstances can obtain a free credit report. *See* FCRA §§ 609, 612. If consumers are not entitled to a free report, they may purchase one for a statutorily capped fee. FCRA § 612(f). The current maximum fee is $10.00. See 70 Fed. Reg. 74,816 (Dec. 16, 2005).

[68] CDIA Communication 01/12/05, *supra* note 55, at 2.

[69] CDIA Communication 01/07/05, *supra* note 15.

[70] The consumers who said they disputed information in their credit files reported that they had disputed to the following entities: 32% to a CRA only; 29% to the creditor only; 30% to both a CRA and the creditor; 6% to an agency other than a CRA or the creditor; and 3% did not know. 2005 GAO Report, *supra* note 63, at 67.

[71] 2005 GAO Report, *supra* note 63, at 30–31.

[72] The Board examined the credit records of a large, nationally representative sample of individuals as of June 30, 2003. This sample was previously examined in detail by the Board as part of a series of articles about the credit reporting system. *See* 2003 FRB Study, *supra* note 22, at 47–73; 2004 FRB Study, *supra* note 11, at 297–322.

[73] *See* appendix C, table 1. With respect to different types of credit accounts, the following percentages of accounts were in dispute: 0.37% of credit card accounts; 0.02% of mortgage loans; 0.0% of auto loans; and 0.04% of other types of credit accounts (such as charge accounts, lines of credit, secured credit, and student loans).

[74] *See* appendix C, table 3.

[75] *See* appendix C, table 2.

[76] FCRA § 611(a)(1)(A). If the consumer submits additional information relevant to the reinvestigation during the thirty-day period, the reinvestigation period can be extended for an additional fifteen days. FCRA § 611(a)(1)(B). In addition, the FACT Act provides that CRAs have forty-five days to complete a reinvestigation if the consumer disputes information after receiving an annual free file disclosure pursuant to the FACT Act. FCRA § 612(a)(3), amended by FACT Act § 211.

[77] FCRA § 611(a)(4).

[78] *Compare* section 611(a)(1)(A) of 1996 FCRA ("the agency shall reinvestigate free of charge") *with* section 611(a)(1)(A) of the FACT Act FCRA ("the agency shall, free of charge, conduct a reasonable reinvestigation").

[79] *Compare* Cushman v. TransUnion Corp., 115 F.3d 220, 225 (3d Cir. 1997) (where a consumer alerted CRA to possible fraud, it was not sufficient for CRA to rely merely on the creditor's information; court applied a two-factor test: (1) whether the consumer has alerted CRA to possibility that source may be unreliable or CRA itself knows or should know that source is unreliable, and (2) cost of verifying accuracy of source compared with possible harm inaccurately reported information may cause consumer); Pinner v. Schmidt, 805 F.2d 1258, 1262 (5th Cir. 1986) (unreasonable for CRA only to contact the creditor's agent to re-verify a delinquent account balance reported on the consumer's credit report where plaintiff notified CRA of his personal dispute with the agent); Soghomonian v. U.S., 278 F. Supp. 2d 1151, 1156 (E.D. Cal. 2003) (CRA does not act reasonably by deferring entirely to another source of information, especially in cases where source on which CRA relies does not consider information supplied by consumers in course of verifying information); *with* Bagby v. Experian Information Systems, 162 Fed. Appx. 600, 606-07 (7th Cir. 2006) (CRA had no duty to perform independent investigation where the consumer provided no evidence that source providing information to CRA was unreliable and cost of investigation far outweighed harm to the consumer); Cahlin v. General Motors Acceptance Corp., 936 F.2d 1151, 1160 (11th Cir. 1991) (CRA's reinvestigation was not unreasonable where CRA exercised independent professional judgment, based on full information, as to how particular account should be reported on credit report and where there was no factual deficiency in credit report); Stewart v. Credit Bureau, Inc., 734 F.2d 47, 55 (D.C. Cir. 1984) (CRA's failure, following reinvestigation of disputed items in credit report, to note that a lien was against the consumer as a business entity, rather than as an individual, and that the consumer contested the lien, did not render report fundamentally incomplete, so as to serve as basis for the consumer's claim that reinvestigation procedures were inadequate to reasonably ensure accurate correction of disputed items); Kettler v. CSC Credit Serv., Inc., 2003 U.S. Dist. LEXIS 14424, *7-8 (D. Minn. Aug. 12, 2003) (where the consumer did not provide specific information regarding nature of inaccuracies in her credit report, court ruled that CRA may rely on information in public records absent more specific evidence that the information is inaccurate).

[80] Comment of consumer groups, at 6.

[81] CDIA Communication 01/12/05, *supra* note 55, at 3. CDIA added that CRAs "also keep in mind that credit repair [organizations] can and do submit falsified documents, including forged letters from credit grantors which advise a consumer reporting agency to delete accurate information." *Id.*

[82] Comment of TransUnion, at 5.

[83] FCRA § 611(a)(2).

[84] *See*, e.g., www.transunion.com, "Dispute"; www.equifax.com, "Online Dispute"; www.experian.com, "Submit a Dispute Online."

[85] FCRA section 623(a)(2) requires that if a furnisher determines that information the furnisher has reported to a CRA is incomplete or inaccurate, the furnisher (1) must promptly notify the CRA of that determination and provide any information necessary for the CRA to make the information complete and accurate and (2) may not furnish the incomplete or inaccurate information to the CRA in the future.

[86] *See* CDIA, "What Is e-OSCAR?" at www.e-oscar.org.

[87] *Id.* Because e-OSCAR is web-based, furnishers are able to avoid the cost of purchasing and updating software. CDIA, "Benefits," www.e-oscar.org/benefits. FCRA section 611(a)(5)(D) requires the nationwide CRAs to implement an automated system through which furnishers may report the results of their investigations to all nationwide CRAs to which the furnishers reported the disputed information. The e-OSCAR system permits such reporting by furnishers.

[88] Comment of CDIA, at 5; Comment of TransUnion, at 4; CDIA Communication 01/12/05, *supra* note 55, at 2.

[89] "Credit repair organizations" generally offer to remove, or assist consumers in removing, derogatory information from consumers' credit files. *See* 15 U.S.C. § 1679b(3) (defining "credit repair organization"). Because of deceptive practices used by many credit repair organizations, Congress enacted the Credit Repair Organizations Act, 15 U.S.C. §§ 1679-1679j, in 1996. TransUnion estimates that between 12% and 20% of all requests for reinvestigations are generated by credit repair organizations. Comment of TransUnion, at 8. Two furnishers, on the other hand, asserted that few, if any, disputes they received came from credit repair organizations. Comment of Coalition, at page 4 of Coalition's attachment; Comment of Zions, at 1.

[90] CDIA Communication 01/12/05, *supra* note 55, at 2.

[91] *Id.* TransUnion estimates that approximately 86% of its dispute notices are sent to e-OSCAR participants; the remaining 14% are sent to paper-based furnishers. Comment of TransUnion, at 6.

[92] CDIA Communication 01/12/05, *supra* note 55, at 3.

[93] *Id.* at 2.

[94] Resellers are discussed in more detail in section II.A of this report.

[95] Comment of NCRA, at 2. As discussed more fully in section IV.D.2, NCRA commented that furnishers vary in the degree to which they cooperate when resellers convey consumer disputes to them.

[96] Comment of CDIA, at 2; Comment of TransUnion, at 4; Comment of Equifax, at 4; Comment of MBA, at 10.

[97] Comment of MBA, at 3.

[98] Comment of Ford County Bank, at 1. Similarly, in the course of a Federal Reserve bank examination, a state member bank stated that because it received so few disputes, it decided not to pay the fee to correct information with the CRA. Furnishers that participate in e-OSCAR are charged $0.25 each time they receive an ACDV or send an AUD. They pay a minimum charge of $21 each quarter, regardless of the number of e-OSCAR transactions they conduct during that period. CDIA, "e- OSCAR Costs," at www.e-oscar.org/costs.htm.

[99] Comment of Ford County Bank, at 1. *See* FCRA § 611(a)(5)(A).

[100] Comment of MBA, at 11.

[101] FCRA § 611(a)(2)(A).

[102] Comment of consumer groups, at 2, 5–6.

[103] Comment of consumer groups, at 7.

[104] Comment of BB&T, at 6; Comment of MBA, at 9; Comment of Wells Fargo, at 5; Comment of ABA, at 4; Comment of Zions, at 4; Comment of Coalition, at 2–3; Comment of MBNA, at 3–4.

[105] Comment of Coalition, at 2. The Coalition recommended that several of these catch-all dispute codes be made more precise. *Id.* The Coalition noted, however, that those members that addressed whether the information from the CRAs is sufficient to conduct an investigation reported that the information is almost always sufficient. *Id.* at 4.

[106] Comment of Coalition, at 1; Comment of MBNA, at 2; Comment of Ford County Bank, at 1; Comment of ABA, at 4; Comment of Wells Fargo, at 5; Comment of Juniper, at 4.

[107] CDIA Communication 01/12/05, *supra* note 55, at 2 n.2.

[108] Comment of MBA, at 9.

[109] Comment of CDIA, at 7. The courts that have addressed the issue of whether the ACDV system and its use of codes to convey the relevant consumer information complies with the FCRA have concluded that, at least in concept, it does. *See* Davis v. Equifax Information Services LLC, 346 F. Supp. 2d 1164, 1176 (N.D. Ala. 2004) (where consumer did not know what information CRA asked furnisher to investigate and consumer's only evidence that CRA failed to convey "all relevant information" to furnisher was fact that CRA conveyed the information electronically, court granted summary judgment for CRA); Perry v. Experian Info. Solutions, No. 05C1578, 2005 U.S. Dist. LEXIS 26040, *22-23 (N.D. Ill. Oct. 28, 2005) (based on scant information in consumer's dispute letters, CRA's

reinvestigation using ACDVs was reasonable); and Lee v. Experian Info. Solutions, No. 02C8424, 2003 U.S. Dist. LEXIS 17420, at 19–20 (N.D. Ill. Oct. 2, 2003) ("[T]he CDV procedure alone is accepted by courts as an adequate method both for assuring accuracy and for reinvestigation" (citing Dickens v. TransUnion Corp., 18 Fed. Appx. 315, 319 (6th Cir. 2001))). Several courts, however, have found that under particular circumstances, the CRA should take additional steps to override or correct the standard procedures when it knows or should know those procedures are not functioning properly in that case. *See* Apodaca v. Discover Financial Services, 2006 U.S. Dist. LEXIS 12505, *32 (D.N.M. Mar. 2, 2006) (where potential harm to the consumer is great and the consumer provides specific and detailed information, a rational factfinder may find this "weigh[s] strongly in favor of investing the resources necessary to complete a more thorough investigation that goes beyond the minimal CDV procedure," which the CRA knew would be inadequate to correct the problems created by its reporting procedures); and Soghomonian v. U.S., 278 F. Supp. 2d 1151, 1157 n.3 (E.D. Cal. 2003) (CRA acted unreasonably in failing to provide furnisher with copy of IRS document supplied by the plaintiffs that proved the plaintiffs' tax lien had been extinguished). Thus, the issue of whether the CRA has conveyed "all relevant information" is a fact-dependent one.

[110] Comment of TransUnion, at 6; Comment of Equifax, at 7.

[111] CDIA Communication 01/12/05, *supra* note 55, at 3 n.4.

[112] Comment of CDIA, at 6. CDIA's members report that they do not have a tracking mechanism that allows them to report on how many written disputes are submitted using only a standardized form and how many contain additional documentation. CDIA Communication 01/12/05, *supra* note 55, at 3.

[113] Comment of TransUnion, at 6.

[114] Comment of CDIA, at 7.

[115] Comment of TransUnion, at 5.

[116] Comment of Equifax, at 7.

[117] Communication from CDIA to the Division of Privacy & Identity Protection, Federal Trade Commission (Apr. 14, 2006) (on file with the Division of Privacy & Identity Protection). Among other things, CDIA noted that some consumers submit disputes with information about different accounts and furnishers commingled, and that it was unclear whether individual furnishers should be permitted to *see* information other than that which relates to their account. According to CDIA, masking or editing consumer documents to maintain privacy would be technologically difficult. In its original comment letter, CDIA had stated that under the e-OSCAR system, "it has become feasible to consider some additional enhancements to an already successful technology. Discussions have begun on a means of delivering or making available consumer documentation, submitted to a consumer reporting agency along with a dispute, to data furnishers to ensure that a furnisher can more fully consider a consumer's dispute." Comment of CDIA, at 5.

[118] FCRA § 623(b)(1). The FACT Act imposes additional duties on furnishers, described in appendix E of this report.

[119] Examples of courts ruling that a furnisher's investigation was sufficient include Westra v. Credit Control of Pinellas, 409 F.3d 825, 827 (7th Cir. 2005) (investigation was reasonable where CRA did not inform furnisher that plaintiff was victim of identity theft and furnisher verified name, address, and date of birth of account and reported to CRA that account belonged to plaintiff); Malm v. Household Bank, N.A., 2004 U.S. Dist. LEXIS 12981, *14-15 (D. Minn. July 7, 2004) (where CRA's CDV stated only "Not his/hers. Provide complete ID" and did not specify that plaintiff believed account belonged to ex-wife only, or that she forged his signature to open it, furnisher conducted reasonable investigation by verifying that plaintiff's personal information matched its records and updating account balance; furnisher did not have to review the actual credit card application). Other courts, however, have ruled that a furnisher's investigation was or might have been insufficient. *See, e.g.*, Johnson v. MBNA, 357 F.3d 426, 431-32 (4th Cir. 2004) (upholding jury verdict finding

that credit card issuer's investigation was not reasonable where company was notified that consumer disputed that she was co-obligor on the account and company reviewed only information in its computerized customer information system and did not consult underlying documents, such as account applications); Schaffhausen v. Bank of America, 393 F. Supp. 2d 853, 858 (D. Minn. 2005) ("Bank of America's convoluted and inconsistent responses to the CRAs' inquiries … create at least a jury question as to the reasonableness of BOA's procedures."); Bruce v. First U.S.A. Bank, 103 F. Supp. 2d 1135, 1143 (E.D. Mo. 2000) (court held that standard for reasonable investigation for furnishers is analogous to that of CRAs, and found issues of material fact where furnisher reviewed only its internal records, which revealed that signature on credit application did not match plaintiff's signature, and furnisher did not contact either the plaintiff or his ex-wife regarding allegations of fraud).

[120] Comment of consumer groups, at 4 (emphasis in original). NAMB reported that in some cases, instead of confirming that the furnisher cannot validate the information, the furnisher will do nothing, or actually report back to the CRA that the information is accurate as reported. Comment of NAMB, at 4. NAMB also commented that there are times when the furnisher is, in fact, given conclusive information about the disputed information, but the corrections or modifications reported back to the CRA are not accurate—e.g., discharge dates are reported inaccurately or balances are not indicated accurately as zero. *Id.*

[121] Comment of consumer groups, at 4.

[122] Comment of Wells Fargo, at 4; Comment of MBA, at 6–7, 9; Comment of Juniper, at 4; Comment of Zions, at 4.

[123] Comment of Wells Fargo, at 5.

[124] Comment of Zions, at 4.

[125] *Id.* at 3.

[126] Comment of MBA, at 10; Comment of Wells Fargo, at 6; Comment of Zions, at 5; Comment of Juniper, at 4–5; Comment of BB&T, at 7; Comment of CDIA, at 7.

[127] Comment of MBA, at 10.

[128] Comment of NAMB, at 3, 6.

[129] FCRA § 623(b)(1)(E), added by FACT Act § 314.

[130] Comment of Juniper, at 5; Comment of BB&T, at 7; Comment of Wells Fargo, at 6; Comment of CDIA, at 7; Comment of Equifax, at 7; Comment of TransUnion, at 7.

[131] Comment of MBA, at 10; Comment of Wells Fargo, at 6; Comment of Zions, at 5; Comment of Juniper, at 4–5; Comment of BB&T, at 7; Comment of BECU, at 3; Comment of CDIA, at 7; Comment of TransUnion, at 7.

[132] CDIA Resource Guide, *supra* note 56, at 14-3; CDIA, "e-OSCAR Benefits," at www.e-oscar.org/benefitsm; Comment of Equifax, at 3. As noted above, the FCRA was amended in 1996 to require nationwide CRAs to implement an automated system through which furnishers may report the results of their investigations to all nationwide CRAs to which the furnisher reported the disputed information. FCRA § 611(a)(5)(D).

[133] CDIA Resource Guide, *supra* note 56, at 14-3.

[134] Comment of MBA, at 10.

[135] Comment of NCRA, at 2.

[136] FCRA § 611(f), added by FACT Act § 316.

[137] Comment of MBA, at 11; Comment of BECU, at 4; Comment of Juniper, at 5.

[138] FCRA § 611(b).

[139] Comment of ABA at 4; Comment of Zions, at 5. However, Juniper stated that these post-investigation dispute statements are not very helpful to consumers, because credit scoring models do not take the statements into account. Comment of Juniper, at 3. A leading producer of credit scoring models, Fair Isaac Corp., reported that, although its scoring models do not take post- investigation dispute statements into consideration when calculating "FICO scores," the models do consider disputes that are still being investigated. The Fair Isaac representative added that some lenders may choose to consider post-

investigation statements in their credit decisions. E-mail from Karlene E. Bowen, Director-Client Relationships, Fair Isaac Corp., to the Division of Financial Practices, Federal Trade Commission (Jan. 12, 2005, 23:32 EST) (on file with the Division of Privacy & Identity Protection).

[140] Comment of TransUnion, at 7. As noted in section IV.A, CDIA reported that 21.8% of the file disclosures issued by the repositories to consumers in 2003 led to a reinvestigation by one of the repositories.

[141] 2005 GAO Report, *supra* note 63, at 67–68.

[142] Comment of CDIA, at 6.

[143] Comment of Equifax, at 7; Comment of CDIA, at 6; Comment of Wells Fargo, at 5.

[144] Comment of CDIA, at 3.

[145] Communication from CDIA to the Division of Financial Practices, Federal Trade Commission (Feb. 2, 2005) (on file with the Division of Privacy & Identity Protection).

[146] Comment of Wells Fargo, at 5; Comment of BECU, at 4; Comment of Zions, at 4. *See also* Comment of Coalition, at 5 and pages 8–9 of Coalition's attachment; Comment of MBNA, at 5; Comment of MBA, at 6, 9 (which mentions disputes communicated by paper).

[147] Comment of Coalition, at 5; Comment of MBNA, at 5.

[148] Comment of consumer groups, at 5.

[149] The FCRA mandates that CRAs modify or delete disputed information if the furnisher does not verify it within the thirty- day reinvestigation period. FCRA § 611(a)(5)(A). *See also* Comment of BECU, at 3; Comment of Juniper, at 4; Comment of CDIA, at 6.

[150] Comment of TransUnion, at 5.

[151] 2005 GAO Report, *supra* note 63, at 32.

[152] *Id.* at 32, 67. If an item is deleted from a consumer's file because a reinvestigation finds that the item is inaccurate, incomplete, or could not be verified, the CRA may not reinsert the item in the consumer's file unless the entity that furnished the item certifies that the item is complete and accurate and the CRA notifies the consumer of the reinsertion. FCRA § 611(a)(5)(B). CRAs also must maintain reasonable procedures designed to prevent the reappearance of previously deleted items in a consumer's file and in consumer reports issued about the consumer. FCRA § 611(a)(5)(C).

[153] Communication from CDIA to the Division of Financial Practices, Federal Trade Commission (Oct. 26, 2004) (on file with the Division of Privacy & Identity Protection).

[154] Statement of Stuart K. Pratt, *supra* note 28, at 14.

[155] *Id.*

[156] TransUnion reported that it does not treat as "repeats" disputes containing additional information, or those made after a reasonable length of time has passed since the last dispute. Comment of TransUnion, at 7.

[157] Comment of TransUnion, at 7.

[158] 2005 GAO Report, *supra* note 63, at 67.

[159] Comment of Coalition, at 3 and page 5 of attachment; Comment of MBNA, at 4; Comment of Wells Fargo, at 2; Comment of BB&T, at 4; Comment of ABA, at 2; Comment of MBA, at 6; Comment of Juniper, at 1; Comment of Zions, at 2 (regarding its mortgages). Zions, for example, reported that its Consumer Loan Servicing Department receives 60% of its disputes through CRAs, 20% directly from consumers, and 20% from internal requests. Comment of Zions, at 1. On the other hand, some furnishers suggested that a higher percentage of their disputes came from consumers. BECU reported that it received only half of its disputes through CRAs and the other half directly from consumers. Comment of BECU, at 1. One community bank in the Coalition's survey reported that 100% of the disputes it receives come directly from consumers. Comment of Coalition, at page 5 of attachment.

[160] *See* FCRA § 623(a)(8), added by FACT Act § 312(c).

[161] FCRA § 623(a)(2).

[162] Comment of Coalition, at 3; Comment of MBNA, at 4; Comment of Wells Fargo, at 2; Comment of Juniper, at 2. The FCRA currently does not require furnishers to provide consumers with a specific address for submitting disputes, but furnishers that provide such an address are exempt from certain kinds of liability under the FCRA. *See* FCRA § 623(a)(1). In addition, as required by the FACT Act, the FTC and the federal financial regulators will promulgate rules that will require consumers who wish to submit disputes directly to furnishers to do so at "the address specified by the [furnisher] for such notices." *See* FCRA § 623(a)(8)(D), added by FACT Act § 312.

[163] Comment of Juniper, at 2.

[164] Comment of Wells Fargo, at 2.

[165] Comment of ABA, at 2; Comment of MBA, at 2.

[166] Comment of ABA, at 2; Comment of BB&T, at 2; Comment of Ford County Bank, at 1.

[167] Comment of MBA, at 6–8; Comment of BECU, at 1–2; Comment of ABA, at 2–3; Comment of Wells Fargo, at 2–5; Comment of Juniper, at 3; Comment of BB&T, at 4; Comment of Zions, at 2.

[168] Comment of MBA, at 6–7; Comment of ABA, at 3; Comment of Wells Fargo, at 2; Comment of Zions, at 2; Comment of Juniper, at 2; Comment of BECU, at 2–3; Comment of BB&T, at 4.

[169] Comment of MBA, at 6–7; Comment of Wells Fargo, at 2. As described above, the consumer groups maintain that furnishers typically are not consulting underlying documents when investigating disputes. *See supra* section IV.D.1.

[170] Comment of MBA, at 7; Comment of Zions, at 2.

[171] Comment of MBA, at 6–7; Comment of Juniper, at 2; Comment of Zions, at 3; Comment of BB&T, at 4. As described above, NAMB reports that some furnishers are not correcting the information in their own records. *See supra* note 126 and accompanying text.

[172] Comment of BECU, at 2–3; Comment of MBA, at 6–7; Comment of Zions, at 2.

[173] Comment of ABA, at 2–3; Comment of Wells Fargo, at 2; Comment of Juniper, at 2; Comment of BB&T, at 4; Comment of Zions, at 2; Comment of MBA, at 6; Comment of BECU, at 2.

[174] Comment of MBA, at 7; Comment of Juniper, at 2; Comment of Zions, at 3.

[175] Comment of Coalition, at 3–4. Wells Fargo commented that up to 25% of disputes it receives directly from consumers do not contain sufficient relevant information to conduct a proper investigation. Comment of Wells Fargo, at 3.

[176] Comment of Coalition, at 3–4; Comment of MBNA, at 4–5; Comment of ABA, at 3; Comment of BECU, at 2; Comment of Zions, at 3. Some commenters suggested that one reason consumers may not provide full information is that credit reports typically do not show the full account number on specific accounts. Comment of NAMB, at 8; Comment of Zions, at 3.

[177] Comment of MBA, at 7. Zions explained that it uses a service available through Experian, called "Bullseye," to obtain information on individual accounts. Comment of Zions, at 3.

[178] Comment of Juniper, at 2; Comment of ABA, at 3; Comment of Coalition, at 3–4; Comment of MBNA, at 4–5; Comment of MBA, at 7.

[179] Comment of consumer groups, at 2.

[180] *Id.*

[181] *Id.* at 9.

[182] *Id.*

[183] *Id.*

[184] *Id.* at 8–10.

[185] *Id.* at 10.

[186] Certain furnishers also maintained that obtaining correction of erroneous information was difficult. Comment of Coalition, at page 11 of Coalition's attachment; Comment of MBA, at 3.

[187] Comment of California Association of Realtors, at 3.

[188] Comment of MBA, at 12. According to CDIA, the "Remarks" field on the ACDV form does allow furnishers to convey certain additional information (e.g., that the account is being paid under a partial payment agreement or has been closed due to transfer) through codes describing the status of the accounts at issue. Communication from CDIA to the Division of Privacy & Identity Protection, Federal Trade Commission (July 21, 2006) (on file with the Division of Privacy & Identity Protection), at 1.

[189] Comment of Coalition, at 1, 4; Comment of MBNA, at 2, 5; Comment of ABA, at 1–2, 4–5; Comment of Wells Fargo, at 6; Comment of Juniper, at 5; Comment of Visa, at 3–5; Comment of CDIA, at 7; Comment of TransUnion, at 7–9.

[190] Comment of Visa, at 4–5.

[191] *Id.* at 4.

[192] *Id.* at 3; Comment of Juniper, at 5. The National Association of Realtors, a trade group representing realtors, suggested shortening the reinvestigation period from thirty days in light of the increased use of technology and the consolidation of CRAs. This trade group suggested that shortening the reinvestigation period would force the CRAs to complete their reinvestigations faster, which would minimize the adverse impacts on consumers caused by incorrect information in their credit histories. Comment of National Association of Realtors, at 2–3. The consumer groups commented, however, that the length of time CRAs and furnishers take to complete reinvestigations usually is not a problem, because they ordinarily are finished quickly through the e-OSCAR system. Comment of consumer groups, at 5.

[193] Comment of Juniper, at 5; Comment of MBA, at 4; Comment of TransUnion, at 8. MBA and TransUnion suggested that changes should be made to curb these types of abuses. MBA suggested that limits should be placed on the number of disputes allowed to be filed by a consumer or credit repair organization within the investigation time period on the same issue on the same trade-line. Comment of MBA, at 11. *See also* Comment of BECU, at 4. TransUnion suggested expanding the definition of "credit repair organization" in the Credit Repair Organizations Act (CROA), 15 U.S.C. sections 1679-1679j, to include not-for-profit agencies and professional associations that advertise their credit repair or counseling services. CROA is intended to protect consumers from deceptive and abusive practices by companies engaged in credit repair. According to TransUnion, amending the definition of "credit repair organization" in this way would give consumers, CRAs, and furnishers a private right of action to enforce their rights under CROA against these entities. Comment of TransUnion, at 8.

[194] Comment of Visa, at 3.

[195] Comment of Juniper, at 5.

[196] Comment of Coalition, at 4; Comment of MBNA, at 5.

[197] Comment of TransUnion, at 7.

[198] FCRA § 621. Other entities, such as the individual states, the U.S. Department of Transportation, and the U.S. Department of Agriculture, also have FCRA enforcement authority under certain circumstances.

[199] FCRA § 621(a).

[200] *See, e.g.*, United States v. Far West Credit, Inc., Civ. No. 2:06CV00041-TC (D. Utah 2006) (consent decree settling charges that reseller failed to follow reasonable procedures to ensure the accuracy of its reports); First American Real Estate Solutions, LLC, 127 F.T.C. 85 (1999) (consent order with reseller concerning the reinvestigation obligations of CRAs). The FTC also settled cases with the three repositories, charging that they failed to establish a toll-free number with "personnel accessible" during normal business hours to answer consumers' questions about their consumer reports, as mandated by FCRA section 609(c)(1). The complaints in these cases alleged that the repositories failed to maintain adequate personnel, resulting in busy signals, excessive hold times, and the blocking of consumer calls from particular locations. The orders require the repositories to maintain adequate personnel, establish auditing requirements to ensure future compliance, and pay a

total of $2.5 million in civil penalties. *See* FTC v. Equifax Credit Info. Services, Inc., No. 1:00-CV-0087 (N.D. Ga. 2000); FTC v. Experian Mktg. Info. Solutions, Inc., No. 3-00CV0056-L (N.D. Tex. 2000); FTC v. TransUnion LLC, 00C 0235 (N.D. Ill. 2000); *see also* United States v. Equifax Credit Info. Servs., Inc., Civ. No. 1:0-CV-0087-MHS (N.D. Ga. 2003) ($250,000 disgorgement remedy for alleged violation of consent decree).

[201] *See* FTC v. NCO Group, Inc., 2004 WL 1103323 (E.D. Pa. 2004) (providing inaccurate delinquency dates; $1.5 million civil penalty); United States v. Fairbanks Capital Corp., Civ. Action No. 03-12219 DPW (D. Mass 2003) (furnishing information to a CRA knowing, or consciously avoiding knowing, that the information is inaccurate); FTC v. DC Credit Servs., Inc., No. 02-5115 (C.D. Cal. 2002) (furnishing information to a CRA knowing, or consciously avoiding knowing, that the information is inaccurate, failing to notify and provide corrections to CRAs when previously reported information was found to be inaccurate, failing to provide accurate delinquency dates, failing to report accounts as "disputed"; $300,000 civil penalty); FTC v. Performance Capital Mgmt., Inc., 2:01cv1047 (C.D. Cal. 2000) (providing inaccurate delinquency dates, failing to properly investigate disputes, failing to report accounts as "disputed"; $2 million civil penalty). All these cases were settlements resulting in consent decrees.

[202] The Federal Reserve System regulates, among others, state-chartered banks that are members of the System. The FDIC regulates, among others, insured state-chartered banks that are not members of the Federal Reserve System.

[203] The OCC regulates national banks.

[204] The FTC announced the program on April 23, 2004. *See* www.ftc.gov/opa/2004/04/cra.htm. The affiliates are discussed in more depth in section II.A.

[205] *See supra* notes 79 and 117 and accompanying text.

[206] *See supra* notes 35-39 and accompanying text. *See also* appendix E.

[207] Source: Consumer Data Industry Association.

[208] Source: Federal Reserve Board.

[209] Source: Consumer Data Industry Association.

[210] FCRA § 611(a)(1)(A), as amended by FACT Act § 317.

[211] FCRA § 611(a)(5)(A), as amended by FACT Act § 314.

[212] FCRA § 612(a)(3), as amended by FACT Act § 211.

[213] FCRA § 611(f), as amended by FACT Act § 316. FCRA section 603(u) defines a "reseller" as a CRA that "assembles and merges" information contained in the database of a repository.

[214] FCRA § 611(f)(2), as amended by FACT Act § 316.

[215] FCRA § 611(a)(1)(A), as amended by FACT Act § 317.

[216] FCRA § 611(f)(3)(A), as amended by FACT Act § 316.

[217] FCRA § 611(f)(3)(B), as amended by FACT Act § 316. Resellers still are free to conduct their own reinvestigations of consumer disputes, but they are no longer required to do so. See FCRA § 611(f)(4), as amended by FACT Act § 316(b).

[218] FCRA § 623(a)(8), as amended by FACT Act § 312(c). When completed, the regulations will be available at www.ftc.gov/credit and www.federalreserve.gov.

[219] FCRA § 623(b)(1)(E), as amended by FACT Act § 314.

[220] FCRA § 623(a)(6), as amended by FACT Act § 154(a) A furnisher may re-report the information if the furnisher subsequently knows or is informed by the consumer that the information is correct. FCRA § 623(a)(6)(B), as amended by FACT Act § 154(a).

[221] FCRA § 623(a)(1)(A) of 1996 FCRA.

[222] FCRA § 623(a)(1)(A), as amended by FACT Act § 312(b)(1). If a furnisher clearly and conspicuously supplies an address to which disputes should be sent, however, this duty does not apply to the furnisher. FCRA § 623(a)(1)(C).

[223] FCRA § 623(a)(1)(D), as amended by FACT Act § 312(b)(2).

[224] FCRA § 623(a)(7), as amended by FACT Act § 217. The financial institution may choose to convey this notice before furnishing the information to the CRA. 12 C.F.R. pt. 222 app. B.

[225] FCRA § 623(e), as amended by FACT Act § 312(a). The FACT Act amendments also added several other furnisher provisions that are not discussed here.

INDEX

D

E

F

G

H

I

J

L

M

N

O

T

U

V

W

Y